DISCOVERY GUIDE

# DEATH & RESURRECTION

## OF THE MESSIAH

## The Faith Lessons™ Series
## with Ray Vander Laan

# DISCOVERY GUIDE
# DEATH & RESURRECTION
## OF THE MESSIAH

THAT THE WORLD MAY KNOW®

**10 FAITH LESSONS BY**

# RAY VANDER LAAN

*with Stephen & Amanda Sorenson*

**ZONDERVAN®**  FOCUS ON THE FAMILY.

ZONDERVAN.com/
AUTHORTRACKER
*follow your favorite authors*

09 10 11 12 13 14 15 • 25 24 23 22 21 20 19 18 17 16 15 14 13 12 11 10 9 8 7 6 5 4 3 2

# CONTENTS

# INTRODUCTION

Because God speaks to us through the Scriptures, studying them is a rewarding experience. Most of the inspired human authors of the Bible, as well as those to whom the words were originally given, were Jews living in the ancient Near East. God's words and actions spoke to them with such power, clarity, and purpose that they wrote them down and carefully preserved them as an authoritative body of literature.

God's use of human servants in revealing himself resulted in writings that clearly bear the stamp of time and place. The message of the Scriptures is, of course, eternal and unchanging — but the circumstances and conditions of the people of the Bible are unique to their times. Consequently, we most clearly understand God's truth when we know the cultural context within which he spoke and acted and the perception of the people with whom he communicated.

This does not mean that God's revelation is unclear if we don't know the cultural context. Rather, by learning how to think and approach life as Abraham, Moses, Ruth, Esther, and Paul did, modern Christians will deepen their appreciation of God's Word. To fully apply the message of the Bible to our lives, we must enter the world of the Bible and familiarize ourselves with its culture.

That is the purpose of this study. The events and characters of the Bible will be presented in their original settings. Although the DVD segments offer the latest archaeological research, this series is not intended to be a definitive cultural and geographical study of the lands of the Bible. No original scientific discoveries are revealed here. The purpose of this study is to help us better understand God's revealed mission for our lives by enabling us to hear and see his words in their original context.

## Understanding the World of the Bible

More than 3,800 years ago, God spoke to his servant Abraham: "Go, walk through the length and breadth of the land, for I am giving it to you" (Genesis 13:17). From the outset, God's choice of a Hebrew nomad to begin his plan of salvation (that is still unfolding) was linked to the selection of a specific land where his redemptive work would begin. The nature of God's covenant relationship with his people demanded a place where their faith could be exercised and displayed to all nations so that the world would know of *Yahweh*, the true and faithful God.

In the Old Testament, God promised to protect and provide for the Hebrews. He began by giving them Canaan — a beautiful, fertile land where he would shower his blessings upon them. To possess this land, however, the Israelites had to live obediently before God. The Hebrew Scriptures repeatedly link Israel's obedience to God to the nation's continued possession of Canaan, just as they link its disobedience to the punishment of exile (Leviticus 18:24 – 28). When the Israelites were exiled from the Promised Land (2 Kings 18:11), they did not experience God's blessings. Only when they possessed the land did they know the fullness of God's promises.

By New Testament times, the Jewish people had been removed from the Promised Land by the Babylonians due to Israel's failure to live obediently before God (Jeremiah 25:4 – 11). The exile lasted seventy years, but its impact upon God's people was astounding. New patterns of worship developed, and scribes and experts in God's law shaped the new commitment to be faithful to him. The prophets predicted the appearance of a Messiah like King David who would revive the kingdom of the Hebrew people.

Even the Promised Land itself had changed, becoming home to many groups of people whose religious practices, moral values, and lifestyles conflicted with those of the Jews. The land that had been the nation of Judah was called "Palestine" or "Judea" (which means Jewish). The Romans had divided the land into several provinces: Judea, Samaria, and Galilee (the three main divisions during Jesus' time); Gaulanitis, the Decapolis, and Perea (east of the Jordan River); and Idumaea (Edom) and Nabatea (in the south). These further divisions of Israel added to the rich historical and cultural background that God had prepared for the coming of Jesus and the beginning of his church.

Living as God's witnesses took on added difficulty as Greek, Roman, and Samaritan worldviews mingled with that of the Jews. But the mission of God's people did not change. They were still to live so that *the world may know that our God is the true God*.

## Our Purpose

Biblical writers assumed that their readers were familiar with the geography of the ancient Near East. Today, unfortunately, many Christians do not have even a basic geographical knowledge of the region. This study is designed to help solve that problem. We will be studying the people and events of the Bible in their geographical and historical contexts. Once we know the who, what, and where of a Bible story, we will be able to understand the why. By deepening our understanding of God's Word, we will be able to strengthen our relationship with him.

Western Christianity tends to spiritualize the faith of the people of the Bible. Modern Christians do not always do justice to God's desire that his people live faithfully for him in specific places, influencing the cultures around them by their words and actions. Instead of seeing the places to which God called his people as crossroads from which to influence the world, we focus on the glorious destination to which we are traveling as we ignore the world around us. We are focused on the destination, not the journey. We have unconsciously separated our walk with God from our responsibility to the world in which he has placed us.

In one sense, our earthly experience is simply preparation for an eternity in the new "Promised Land." Preoccupation with this idea, however, distorts the mission God has set for us. That mission is the same one he gave to the Israelites: to live obediently *within* the world so that through us, *the world may know that our God is the one true God*.

# WHEN STORMS COME

Water has always been an essential resource for people living in the Middle East. During biblical times, people built cities near fresh water sources such as lakes and springs. They built cisterns, elaborate aqueducts, and even deep tunnels to preserve and utilize this precious liquid. Bible stories often mention events, discussions, and disputes concerning water.

For many people who live in the modern world, water is more than an essential resource for life. We enjoy the beauty and recreational benefits of lakes, oceans, and other bodies of water. We tend to assume that people who lived in the ancient Near East, including Jesus' disciples, viewed large bodies of water in the same way we do. But the ancient Jewish people were descendants of desert nomads. To their way of thinking, this highly valued commodity also had a darker side. Large bodies of water often represented evil, death, and chaos—some of worst things in life.

The Jewish people recognized the beauty of the Sea of Galilee, which is evident in the ancient rabbinic saying, "The Lord has created seven seas, but the Sea of Galilee is his delight." As the largest body of fresh water in Israel, the Sea of Galilee was also an important source of food and provided an efficient means of transportation between the cities surrounding it. But the darker side of the Sea of Galilee was never far from the minds of the Jews who lived nearby. When cool winds blow off the mountains to the east of the Sea of Galilee (what people today call the

Golan Heights), that air sinks rapidly, displacing the warmer air on the surface of the water. This phenomenon causes sudden, severe storms. Because the ancient Jews believed that evil forces caused stormy seas, they viewed such storms with fear. Only God, they believed, could calm the chaos of stormy water because only he could control evil.

It is interesting that Jesus deliberately chose the region on the northern shore of the Sea of Galilee to be the base for his teaching ministry. In this region he called himself "living water" and performed miracles on and near the water. On the surrounding hillsides and along the shore, he taught the crowds who came to hear him, often using fishing imagery to illustrate his message. And from the shores of the Sea of Galilee Jesus called four fishermen — Peter, Andrew, James, and John — to be his disciples.

As they spent time with Jesus, the disciples learned more about who Jesus was and who he had called them to be. They also witnessed his great power over evil, especially when they endured a terrifying nighttime storm on the Sea of Galilee. During that night, Jesus allowed his disciples to strain alone at the oars of their boat for many hours. Stuck in the middle of the Sea of Galilee, rowing against towering waves, they learned much more about faith and the rabbi who came to them walking on the water. There is much for us to learn from this story as well.

## Opening Thoughts (4 minutes)

### The Very Words of God

> Peace I leave with you; my peace I give you. I do not give to you as the world gives. Do not let your hearts be troubled and do not be afraid.
>
> **John 14:27**

### Think About It

Each of us faces difficulties — financial setbacks, serious illness, catastrophic loss of our home or business, loss of significant relationships, legal problems — all of which we could label as "storms" in life.

Which "storms" in life frighten you most deeply? To what extent do you believe evil forces may be involved in some of these "storms"?

## DVD Teaching Notes (16 minutes)

### Perceptions of water

### The disciples' catch

### The disciples' terrifying night

### Peter's courage

## DVD Discussion (7 minutes)

1.   Please refer to the map of the Sea of Galilee on page 15.
     Note the location of Capernaum — the departure point for
     Jesus' disciples — and Bethsaida — their destination. Also
     note Gennesaret, about seven miles away, where they finally
     ended up the next morning.

     Like the disciples, we may at times set off in the direc-
     tion we think God wants us to go but end up in a place we
     never expected him to take us. If you feel comfortable doing
     so, briefly describe a time when you did your best to follow
     Jesus toward a specific goal but ended up in a very different
     situation.

     What about your experience was similar to what the dis-
     ciples experienced?

     What did you learn through that experience about God and
     your walk with him?

2.   Why do you think Jesus allowed his disciples to row against
     the threatening waves for hours without providing relief
     from their frightening situation and difficult labor? What
     might we learn from this?

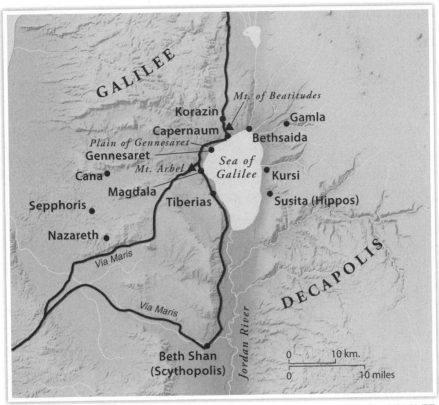

**SEA OF GALILEE**

3. A first-century disciple wanted more than anything else to be like his rabbi. In light of this desire, what do you think went through Peter's mind when he stepped out of the boat and started walking toward Jesus? What might he have been thinking when he started to sink and called out to Jesus for help?

# Small Group Bible Discovery and Discussion (21 minutes)

### Choices of Faith

As we go through life, we will face frightening, difficult "storms" that threaten to overwhelm us. Like Jesus' disciples, we must choose how to respond when we encounter such circumstances. Let's read what the Bible says about the disciples' terrifying night on the Sea of Galilee and then consider the experiences of a few other people who took courageous steps of faith when they faced challenging life storms.

1.  Jesus and his disciples had gone by boat to a quiet place for some much needed rest, but thousands of people followed them, which led to the feeding of the five thousand (Mark 6:34 – 44).

    a.  At the end of the day, what did Jesus have his disciples do, and what did he do? What ideas do you have about why he did this? (See Mark 6:45 – 52.)

    b.  What do you think the disciples were thinking and feeling as they struggled against the wind and waves?

    c.  How did Jesus respond to their cries? What key words did he use, and why do you think he spoke to them as he did?

2. Now read Matthew's account of this story in Matthew 14:25 – 34.

   a. Based on Peter's initial response to Jesus, what can we conclude about his desire to be a disciple of Jesus, to be like his rabbi in every way?

   b. How much courage did it take for Peter to exercise this level of faith?

   c. What did Peter (and the rest of the disciples) doubt and fear, and how did these emotions affect their faith?

3. Just as Peter stepped out of the boat in faith to follow Jesus, we also have the opportunity to follow Jesus and do whatever he asks, no matter how frightening the situation or unknown the result. Following Jesus took the disciples to Gennesaret instead of Bethsaida, and it may take us in entirely new directions — perhaps in our relationships, our careers, or in how we share the gospel message. Read and discuss the following stories from the Bible that highlight people who took steps of courage and faith in their walk with God.

| Scripture Text on Choices of Faith | What courageous steps did the people involved take, and what was their attitude as they stepped forward? | What obstacle(s) that could have shaken their faith did they have to overcome, and where did their step of faith lead? |
|---|---|---|
| Mark 10:46–52 | | |
| John 9:1–7, 24–38 | | |
| Matt. 8:5–13 | | |

## Faith Lesson (6 minutes)

When we face life's inevitable "storms," we can choose to obey and trust God — or we can choose to follow our own path. Just as the disciples cried out to Jesus that night on the stormy Sea of Galilee, we also can cry out to him, step out in faith to follow him, and in turn receive what he provides for those who love him.

1. Given the mind-set of the disciples' culture — the evil that the storm-swept sea represented to them — can you imagine

how terrified they must have been when they first saw Jesus? How would you describe their fear?

Which situations and circumstances in life frighten you?

How do you respond, and where do you turn for help when you come face-to-face with those fears?

2. As you face difficult "storms" that threaten to overwhelm you, which truths about God's character encourage you to persevere?

3. The disciples had seen Jesus' power demonstrated in many ways, yet when Jesus calmed the sea, they exclaimed, "Truly you are the Son of God" (Matthew 14:33).

   a. What have you seen God do that causes you to marvel and worship him?

## FACT FILE
### First-Century Galilean Boat

The replica below shows the type of boat the disciples would have used on the Sea of Galilee. It was reconstructed based on the remains of a first-century boat found buried in the mud of the Sea of Galilee. Imagine what it would have been like to be one of Jesus' disciples during that stormy night!

- The wooden boat is twenty-six feet long and seven and a half feet wide.
- It would have had a crew of five: four members would have rowed at the two pairs of oars, the fifth would have steered. It also carried a small sail.
- The boat could have held several people in addition to the crew.
- A cushion could be placed on the small deck at either end of the boat so a person could sleep there.
- The sides of the boat were low to make it easier to cast nets over the side and draw them in. Waves did not have to be high to threaten the boat!

**GALILEAN BOAT**

b. How has that action of God affected your desire to follow him faithfully?

4. Which courageous step(s) might God be calling you to take today?

## Closing (1 minute)

Please read aloud Psalm 9:10: "Those who know your name will trust in you, for you, Lord, have never forsaken those who seek you." Then pray together, focusing on the awesome love and power of God. Thank him for his commitment to help you face life's storms and for always being faithful and trustworthy. Determine to call out to him quickly when storms erupt in your life. Ask him to help you to not be afraid and to exercise trusting, persevering faith in him.

### Memorize

*Those who know your name will trust in you, for you, Lord, have never forsaken those who seek you.*

*Psalm 9:10*

# When Following Jesus Is the Most Important Thing in Life

*In-Depth Personal Study Sessions*

## Day One | A New Calling

### The Very Words of God

> *As Jesus was walking beside the Sea of Galilee, he saw two brothers, Simon called Peter and his brother Andrew. They were casting a net into the lake, for they were fishermen. "Come, follow me," Jesus said, "and I will make you fishers of men."*
>
> **Matthew 4:18–19**

### Bible Discovery

### *Becoming "Fishers of Men"*

Fishing was an essential occupation for the people who lived near the Sea of Galilee, so it shouldn't surprise us to learn that Jesus used commonly understood images from the world of fishing to communicate to people in that region. In fact, Jesus chose four fishermen to be among his first twelve disciples, and he used the imagery of fishing to communicate the new calling he presented to them. That calling — to follow him and become fishers of men who guide people into a personal relationship with him — is the same calling he presents to us today.

1.  Which region of Israel did Jesus choose as the focal point for his ministry, and why? What was his message? (See Matthew 4:12 – 17, and refer to the map on page 26.)

**DID YOU KNOW?**
The fishing motif was so strong in Jesus' teaching that the Greek word for *fish* (*ichthus*) came to represent Jesus' name. The first letters of the Greek words meaning "Jesus Christ, God's Son, Savior" spell *ichthus*.

2.  As Jesus walked beside the Sea of Galilee, he saw two brothers at work, fishing. What did Jesus ask them to do, and how did they respond? (See Matthew 4:18 – 20; Mark 1:16 – 18.)

3.  Jesus also called out to the two sons of Zebedee who were in a boat working with their father. How did they respond to Jesus' call, and what does their response reveal about their attitude toward Jesus and their commitment to him? (See Matthew 4:21 – 22.)

4.  The four fishermen Jesus called were Peter, Andrew, James, and John.

    a.  In what ways do you think their occupation had prepared them to understand and fulfill the mission Jesus had in store for them — that of becoming "fishers of men"? (See Mark 1:16 – 18; Luke 5:1 – 11.)

    b.  In what way does their response to Jesus' call differ from that of many would-be disciples today? (See Matthew 4:20, 22; Mark 1:18, 20.)

## TWO KINDS OF FISHERMEN

| Fishermen of Galilee | Fishermen of God |
| --- | --- |
| Fishermen used different kinds of nets and methods (seine nets, circular cast nets, trammel nets, hook and line, spears) to catch different kinds of fish (Job 18:8; Ecclesiastes 9:12; Isaiah 19:8; Matthew 17:24 – 27; John 21:6 – 7). | God wants us to use skill, dedication, and care in "fishing" for people who are not yet Christians (Matthew 13:47; Mark 1:16 – 18; Luke 5:10). |
| Fishermen fished in the heat of summer and the cold of winter. They fished from the shore and from boats and at different times of the day to catch different types of fish (John 21:3 – 6; Luke 5:5 – 6). | God wants us to vary the ways in which we, as "fishers of men," do our work of sharing Jesus so that we can guide different types of people into the kingdom of God. |
| Sometimes fishermen caught fish, sometimes they didn't (John 21:3 – 6; Luke 5:5 – 6). | When we share Christ, people sometimes respond to him, but at other times they don't. |
| Fishermen threw away the bad fish they caught (Matthew 13:48). | One day, God's angels will separate the righteous from the unrighteous and throw the unrighteous into the fiery furnace (Matthew 13:49 – 50). |

## Reflection

Today God invites each of us to follow him obediently and to share his love and truth with other people so that they will know who he is and respond to his call. What we say through our actions as well as through our words is the vital message that can help (or hinder) people in our increasingly secular culture to recognize and respond to God.

In what ways is the response of the fishermen Jesus chose to be his disciples similar to or different from your response to Jesus?

What have you learned about Jesus' call to the disciples and their response that prompts you to respond to Jesus more willingly and with a greater level of commitment?

How deep is your commitment to being a disciple of Jesus —

to being like him in every way?

to following where he leads even when it is difficult or frightening?

If you are a Christian, what does it mean for you to be a "fisher of men"?

In which specific way(s) do you demonstrate Jesus' love and truth in your everyday world?

What excuses do you tend to make for not living out Jesus' calling on your life?

## Memorize

*"Love the Lord your God with all your heart and with all your soul and with all your strength and with all your mind"; and, "Love your neighbor as yourself."*

*Luke 10:27*

## DATA FILE
### The Sea of Galilee

Although it is called a "sea," the Sea of Galilee is really a freshwater lake, fed primarily by the Jordan River that flows in from the north.

- More than twelve miles long from north to south and nearly eight miles wide at its widest point, it is the largest body of fresh water in Israel.
- It is more than 150 feet deep in some places, and the surface of the water is nearly 700 feet below sea level.
- It is subject to sudden storms that are caused by cool east winds that blow over the warmer air that covers the surface of the lake. As the heavier cold air drops and the warm air rises, the resulting air turbulence can lead to violent storms.
- It is the locale where Jesus lived and conducted most of his ministry, including ten of his thirty-three recorded miracles.
- It teems with fish today, just as it did during Jesus' time.
- Surrounded by fertile hills and mountains where several hot mineral springs can be found, the sea is deep blue in color.

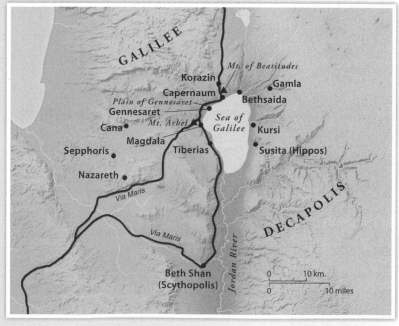

**SEA OF GALILEE**

## **Day Two** | The Dark Side of the Sea

### The Very Words of God

> *Am I the sea, or the monster of the deep, that you put me under guard?*
>
> **Job 7:12**

### Bible Discovery

### *The Sea Represented Evil*

In the minds of the Jewish people during biblical times, the sea symbolized evil — the Abyss, which was the home of Satan and his demons. And many people believed storms were caused by evil forces. So in the Bible, the sea generally represented the forces of evil in much the same way that a shepherd, rock, and living water represented God. People in our contemporary, Western world usually don't attach such symbolic meanings to what we see in nature, but we can better understand the Bible if we take the extra effort to consider the symbolic significance of the sea.

1. The text of the Bible includes many references to the "sea." For each of the following Scriptures, describe how the evil of the "sea" is personified:

    Psalm 74:12 - 14

    Isaiah 27:1

    Daniel 7:2 - 7

Jonah 2:1 – 6

Revelation 13:1 – 9

2.  What is the similarity between the Abyss and the sea? (See Revelation 11:3 – 7; 17:8; 20:1 – 3.)

3.  In Matthew 11:20 – 24, what condemnation did Jesus give to people who lived in Capernaum (at the edge of the sea) and had heard his message but did not repent?

    Given the Jewish perception of the sea as being the evil domain of Satan, how strong a message was Jesus conveying by these words?

4.  Read Luke 8:27 – 33, which records an incident involving Jesus, the forces of evil, and the sea (Abyss).

    a.  When Jesus confronted the demon-possessed man, where did the demons beg Jesus not to send them?

    b.  Where did the demons want to go instead?

    c.   What happened when Jesus gave the demons permission to go there?

5.   What image of the sea did Jude use to describe evil, ungodly people, and what does it communicate to you? (See Jude 13.)

## Reflection

If we watch the sea carefully — its punishing waves, shifting currents, frightening creatures — it's easy to see why ancient people viewed it with suspicion and fear. The symbolic evil of the sea would have been particularly powerful in the minds of the Jewish people whose nomadic roots lay in the firm, rocky wastelands of the desert.

    In which area(s) of life are you being battered by life's "storms"?

    What do you view as the source of these challenges?

    How does your understanding of the source of the storms in your life affect how you deal with them?

When you confront the forces of evil (or chaotic representations of it) in your life, where do you find strength to stand firm against the attack(s)? In other words, where do you place your trust and hope?

Which image from your world best describes your understanding of Satan and his evil work in the world?

Which image do you find to be a helpful symbol and reminder of God's power over evil — his willingness and ability to protect and preserve his faithful followers as they stand against evil?

## Memorize

*But the Lord is faithful, and he will strengthen and protect you from the evil one.... May the Lord direct your hearts into God's love and Christ's perseverance.*

*2 Thessalonians 3:3, 5*

# Day Three | God Is the Deliverer and Tamer of the Sea

## The Very Words of God

*Without warning, a furious storm came up on the lake, so that the waves swept over the boat. But Jesus was sleeping. The disciples went and woke him, saying, "Lord, save us! We're going to drown!" He replied, "You of little faith, why are you so afraid?" Then he got up and rebuked the winds and the waves, and it was completely calm.*

*Matthew 8:24 – 26*

## Bible Discovery

### God Rescues People from Evil

Even though the people of Jesus' day lived on the shores of the Sea of Galilee and worked on it, the sea remained a symbol of evil forces that were present in the world and were opposed to God. The Jews believed that God alone could tame the sea and rescue them from its evil. So when Jesus stilled the storm on the Sea of Galilee and performed miracles in the region, he was revealing more than his divinity and his power over creation; he was demonstrating his power over evil.

1. What do we learn about God's power over water in Genesis 1:2, 6 – 10 and Psalm 24:1 – 2?

2. How has God used his power over water and evil to bring the sinful acts of people to an end? (See Genesis 7:1 – 24; Exodus 14:23 – 28.)

3.  When has God used water to save his people? (See Exodus
    14:5 – 9, 27 – 30; Psalm 77:16 – 20; Isaiah 51:10.)

4.  As you read the following Bible passages, take note of the
    water-related images and terminology the writers used.
    What do their descriptions of what God has done tell you
    about their understanding of the nature of their difficulties
    and what is really at stake?

    Psalm 30:1 – 3

    Psalm 65:5 – 7

    Psalm 69:1 – 3, 13 – 15

    Psalm 89:9

    Jonah 2:1 – 6

## Reflection

Although we in modern culture seldom refer to water as the "Abyss,"
we readily understand the meaning of words such as "deep waters"
or "depths" when they are used to describe times of difficulty,

despair, or attacks by the evil one. Just as Jesus lifted his sinking disciple, Peter, from the storm-tossed waves on the Sea of Galilee, God still rescues his people from evil. We serve the God who is greater than any evil we may face. No circumstance is too difficult for him to overcome, and no depth is beyond his reach or hidden from his ability to save.

Do you believe that God still intervenes miraculously when his people call on him for help? Why or why not?

What experiences in your life have most impacted your willingness or unwillingness to cry out to God when "tumultuous waves" threaten you?

In what ways has God "stilled storms" in your life or lifted someone you know "out of the depths"?

What have you realized about God through these events?

How has your experience affected the way you follow Jesus in your everyday life?

Which "storms" in your life right now need to be tamed by God?

Do you have confidence in his power to save you, and do you trust him to lift you up? If so, in what ways does God's ability to defeat the power of Satan make a difference in how you live? If not, what do you need to do to develop a relationship of trust and confidence in him?

## Memorize

*I will exalt you, O LORD, for you lifted me out of the depths.... O LORD my God, I called to you for help and you ... brought me up from the grave; you spared me from going down into the pit.*

*Psalm 30:1 – 3*

## Day Four | God Uses "Storms" to Teach Us

### The Very Words of God

*Consider it pure joy, my brothers, whenever you face trials of many kinds, because you know that the testing of your faith develops perseverance. Perseverance must finish its work so that you may be mature and complete, not lacking anything.*

*James 1:2 – 4*

### Bible Discovery

### *God Trains Us as We Struggle through Our Trials*

Even though God loves us beyond measure and is always with us, he sometimes allows us to struggle — just as he allowed the disciples to struggle against the waves that stormy night on the Sea of Galilee. Although it may seem to us that God is unaware of (and perhaps unconcerned about) our pain, difficult labor, or grief, nothing could be further from the truth. God is keenly aware of the challenges we face, and he allows them so that we will be "mature and complete, not lacking anything."

As you read the following accounts of struggle from the Bible, think about the role of these "storms" in preparing God's people to fulfill his purposes.

| Scripture Text | What were the people learning about God and his faithfulness (about how to obey him)? | What were they learning about how to persevere in adversity (about how much they needed God's help)? |
|---|---|---|
| Exod. 2:23–3:10; 5:17–6:8 | | |
| Judg. 6:1–16; 8:28 | | |
| 1 Kings 17:7–24 | | |
| 2 Cor. 11:24–29; 12:7–10 | | |

## Reflection

Although the stories of struggle you have just read happened long ago, it's likely that you identify with some of them. Every day, each of us must choose whether or not we will follow where God leads us. Will we take on the difficult challenge God has put before us? Will we call on God and trust him to help us? Will we choose to believe that he will unfold his plans through us? Take some time to make the faith lessons of these stories personal to your life — including your relationship with God.

Which story particularly resonated with you, and why?

As you read these stories, what did *you* realize about God and your relationship with him?

On a scale of one (low) to ten (high), to what extent are you persevering in faith and working to accomplish what God has given you to do?

What is your current struggle, and what are you learning as you persevere through it?

Where do you think this struggle will lead, and what knowledge and skills are you learning that will help you to accomplish what God may want you to do for him?

Imagine your response if Jesus were to walk up to you as you "strain at the oars" of the struggle you are facing. Would you be surprised, frightened, or excited to see him there?

Would you be eager to pursue your challenge to a deeper level as Peter did by walking on the water toward Jesus, or would you cling to the relative safety of the boat? Why?

If Jesus gave you the opportunity to talk with him and share your thoughts and feelings regarding the "storm" with which you are struggling, would you do it? What keeps you from doing this each day, during a quiet time with God?

## DID YOU KNOW?

Even though God is always with us and watching over us, he sometimes allows us to struggle—just as he allowed the disciples to struggle against the waves. God uses storms in our lives to teach us to:

- Depend on him
- Have faith in his plan for our lives
- Call out to him for help
- Remind us that we need him and can't handle everything on our own
- Commit ourselves to practice and persevere in faith—to do whatever it takes to accomplish that which he has called us to do

## Day Five | Seeking God in a Solitary Place

### The Very Words of God

*Jesus went out to a mountainside to pray, and spent the night praying to God.*

*Luke 6:12*

**Bible Discovery**

## *Setting Aside Time with God to Maintain Equilibrium*

In the video for this session, you learned that Jesus sent his disciples out to cross the Sea of Galilee, then went to a solitary place to be alone with his heavenly Father. Jesus often sought solitary places to pray — sometimes alone, sometimes with his disciples; sometimes in the evening, sometimes before dawn. Although Jesus was divine, he was also human, so at times he became physically and emotionally weary just as we do. He needed time with his heavenly Father to regain his strength, refine his focus, seek God's wisdom, and be encouraged.

1. What do you imagine everyday life was like for Jesus as he conducted his ministry in the towns surrounding the Sea of Galilee? Write down the kinds of things you think he did, how long he spent doing them, how many people he saw in an average day.

   Now read Matthew 9:18 – 31. Is this the pace of life and the level of interaction with people you expected of Jesus?

   In what ways might this brief "snapshot" change your picture of the kind of life Jesus actually lived?

2. Why was it vitally important for Jesus to spend time alone with his Father as he faced the following situations?

   Matthew 14:3 – 23

Mark 1:21 – 35

Luke 6:12 – 19

Luke 22:39 – 46

3.  Why did Jesus seek out such "lonely places"? (See Mark 1:40 – 45.)

4.  After spending time alone with his Father, what did Jesus often do? (See Matthew 14:34 – 36; Mark 1:35 – 42.)

## Reflection

Every day each of us encounters challenges and opportunities as we seek to obey God's call. We have opportunities to share love and practical help with needy people, but there are so many needs. We wrestle with issues of sin and selfishness. We get stressed when relationships break down or require more than we can (or want to) give. Juggling — work, family, God, and ministry — takes a toll on us. Jesus, too, experienced a demanding life, but he deliberately set aside time to be with his Father regularly. His practice of spending time in quiet places with his Father illustrates our need to do the same.

Why do you think quiet times with his Father were so important to Jesus?

Do you truly believe that spending time alone with God is essential to your busy life? Why or why not?

When you feel you have nothing left to offer to people who need you, what difference does it make if you spend more time alone with God?

To what extent do you neglect time alone with God, and why?

What happens to you when you neglect solitary time with God?

What's the difference between spending time with God because someone emphasizes its importance and doing it because you want to know God more fully?

Which things tend to hinder your times with God?

Where might you find "lonely places" to be with God, to pray, and to read God's Word? Why are these often hard to find?

What changes might you make in order to have more meaningful times with him?

## Memorize

*Delight yourself in the Lord and he will give you the desires of your heart. Commit your way to the Lord; trust in him and he will do this: He will make your righteousness shine like the dawn, the justice of your cause like the noonday sun. Be still before the Lord and wait patiently for him.*

**Psalm 37:4 – 7**

# PIERCING THE DARKNESS

Jesus came to share the life-giving message of God's kingdom with both Jews and Gentiles. Thus he interacted with many different kinds of people during his ministry — Jews who were satisfied with the Romans; Jewish zealots who hated the Romans; religious Jews; and yes, even pagans who lived in the Decapolis east of the Sea of Galilee. This video gives us a view of Jesus' compassion for people who did not know or honor God, people who had never before experienced the ministry of God in their lives. It also highlights his commitment to actively confront the power of evil in the world.

From the eastern shore of the Sea of Galilee, a district known as the Decapolis spread to the south and east. It originally comprised ten sophisticated cities that had been founded by the Greeks, but by the time of Jesus it had grown to eighteen cities. According to one rabbinic tradition, its inhabitants had descended from the seven Canaanite nations that Joshua drove out of the Promised Land (Joshua 3:10; Acts 13:17 – 19). The historic Canaanite and Hellenistic influences had a powerful stronghold on the Decapolis, making it a thoroughly pagan region. People living there participated in fertility cults and chose the pig, which the Jews considered "unclean," as the animal to be used in their sacred rituals.

Although some Jews lived in the Decapolis, the region was so evil that religious Jews believed that Beelzebub himself lived there. It certainly was not a place God-fearing Jews would choose to visit. To them, the Decapolis was simply the "far country" or the place "across the sea." Yet Jesus went there, and this session will focus on understanding the significance of Jesus' decision to sail across the Sea of Galilee to the Decapolis.

Wherever he went, Jesus — the light of the world — deliberately, righteously, and actively confronted spiritual darkness. His trip to the Decapolis was no exception. That day, Jesus performed at least two miracles:

First, he calmed the furious storm that suddenly came up as they crossed the lake. When he calmed the sea, he was not simply demonstrating his power over creation; he was confronting the power and influence of evil that the sea represented.

Second, Jesus healed a dangerous, demon-possessed man who confronted him as soon as he landed on the eastern shore of the Sea of Galilee (the Decapolis region). Jesus defeated Satan's power by casting the demons from the man into a nearby herd of pigs — the very animals the pagan inhabitants considered to be sacred. The pigs then ran into the lake — the symbol of the Abyss — and drowned. These demonstrations of Jesus' divine power had such a strong impact that the local people pleaded with Jesus to leave their territory.

The man whom Jesus had healed and set free from Satan's demons, however, was a changed man. He wanted to accompany Jesus, but Jesus had something else in mind. Jesus told him to go home and tell other people in the Decapolis what the Lord had done for him.

Evidently the man obeyed. As a result of Jesus' willingness to reach out and save just one man, many pagans in the Decapolis became Christians. In fact, the area became a cornerstone of the early Christian church. Christians from this area played a key role in the early church councils that defined the differences between heresy and orthodox Christian doctrine, and established the canon — the books that we read in the Bible today.

# Opening Thoughts (4 minutes)

## *The Very Words of God*

> *Finally, be strong in the Lord and in his mighty power. Put on the full*
> *armor of God so that you can take your stand against the devil's schemes.*
> *For our struggle is not against flesh and blood, but against the rulers,*
> *against the authorities, against the powers of this dark world and against*
> *the spiritual forces of evil in the heavenly realms.*
>
> *Ephesians 6:10 – 12*

## Think About It

We can all identify places and segments of our culture in which
Satan and his evil influences are particularly active. It can be much
more difficult, however, for us to identify where the light of God is
piercing the spiritual darkness in those arenas.

Which places or segments of culture seem so evil to you that you
don't want anything to do with them? What would be your response
if, just as he did when he took his disciples to visit the Decapolis,
Jesus announced to you, "Today, that's exactly where I want you to
be involved"?

# DVD Teaching Notes (17 minutes)

### The Decapolis

### Feeding the five thousand and the four thousand

**The trip "across the sea"**

**The demon-possessed man**

**Jesus' call to confront evil**

## DVD Discussion (8 minutes)

Look at the map on page 47. Note the area of the Decapolis in relationship to Capernaum and the Sea of Galilee. Also note the locations of Beth Shan and the Decapolis cities near the shore of the Sea of Galilee.

1.   What were the origins (historical and cultural) of the people who lived in the Decapolis?

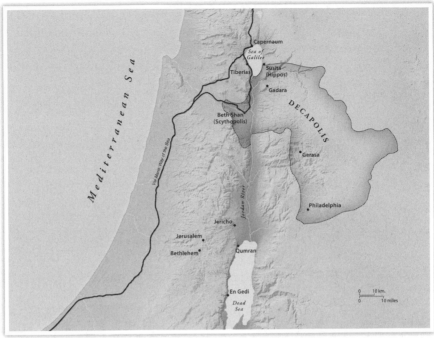

**ISRAEL AND THE DECAPOLIS**

How did the Jews view these people and why?

2.  Why did Jesus sail to the Decapolis? What can we learn from his decision to take his disciples into the most pagan area of his world?

3.  How do you think the disciples felt about going across the Sea of Galilee to "the other side"?

Do you think they were surprised that a demon-possessed man met them almost immediately after Jesus calmed the storm? Why or why not?

4.  As you consider the impact of Jesus' visit to the Decapolis, what have you discovered about the *importance* of one person in the eyes of God? About the *influence* of one person in the hands of God?

## Small Group Bible Discovery and Discussion (19 minutes)

### *Jesus Has Given Us Power to Boldly Confront Evil*

We Christians sometimes choose to ignore the evil around us and hide in our "safe" communities and churches. At other times, we compromise with sin. God, however, calls those who follow him to boldly confront the power of evil wherever it is. He calls us to respond compassionately and appropriately to both personal evil — such as immorality, injustice, and hatred — and natural evil — such as death and disease.

1.  What do Ephesians 6:12 and 1 John 5:19 reveal about the evil one's work in our world?

How seriously do we, as Christians, consider the message of these passages as we go about our daily lives?

What would change — for us individually, and in the world around us — if we were to take this message to heart and live in response to it?

2.  Read the following passages and identify some of the ways in which Satan has tried to derail God's plans:

Esther 3:5 – 11, 13 – 14

Matthew 2:13 – 16

Matthew 4:1 – 11

Matthew 16:21 – 23

Luke 22:3 – 6

3.   How can we know for sure that God's power is greater than
     Satan's power? (See Matthew 13:41 – 43; John 16:33; Romans
     16:20; 2 Corinthians 10:4 – 5; 1 John 4:4, 5:4 – 5.)

To what extent do you believe God's power is at work in
the lives of Christians today? For example, how much do we
value, depend on, and use this power?

What, if anything, about your answer concerns you?

## Faith Lesson (6 minutes)

In many respects, life can be viewed as a spiritual battleground
between good and evil, God and Satan. Just as Jesus took his disciples to the Decapolis and appropriated God's power to confront
and defeat the devil on his own turf, Christians today also are commanded to participate in this battle. When we stand for God in a
culture that does not hold his values, we can expect some people to
resist and resent us — and the message of Christ that we bring.

1.   When you come face-to-face with evil, are you — like the
     disciples — afraid that Jesus will allow you to perish in the
     storm?

If so, why? If not, what is it that you depend on to help you remain strong in the battle against evil?

2. What have you learned today that encourages you to take your place on the spiritual battle lines, or that can help to strengthen your faith and bolster your courage when evil threatens?

3. How would you honestly assess your engagement in the battle against evil? Are you on the "sea" or on the "sidelines"?

Where is it that God wants you to shine his light into the darkness?

Where is it that God wants you to stand for his values?

Where is it that God wants you to set free someone who is trapped by evil?

## Closing (1 minute)

Read together Ephesians 6:10 – 13: "Finally, be strong in the Lord and in his mighty power. Put on the full armor of God so that you can take your stand against the devil's schemes. For our struggle is not against flesh and blood, but against the rulers, against the authorities, against the powers of this dark world and against the spiritual forces of evil in the heavenly realms. Therefore put on the full armor of God, so that when the day of evil comes, you may be able to stand your ground, and after you have done everything, to stand." Then pray, thanking God for Jesus, who is our example in piercing the spiritual darkness that surrounds us. Ask God to prepare and arm you for the battles you will face. Ask him for the courage to confront evil and deliver people who are enslaved by the evil one.

### Memorize

*Finally, be strong in the Lord and in his mighty power. Put on the full armor of God so that you can take your stand against the devil's schemes. For our struggle is not against flesh and blood, but against the rulers, against the authorities, against the powers of this dark world and against the spiritual forces of evil in the heavenly realms. Therefore put on the full armor of God, so that when the day of evil comes, you may be able to stand your ground, and after you have done everything, to stand.*

*Ephesians 6:10 – 13*

# When Following Jesus Is the Most Important Thing in Life

*In-Depth Personal Study Sessions*

## **Day One** | Committed to Confronting Evil

### The Very Words of God

> *Very early in the morning, while it was still dark, Jesus got up, left the house and went off to a solitary place, where he prayed. Simon and his companions went to look for him, and when they found him, they exclaimed: "Everyone is looking for you!" Jesus replied, "Let us go somewhere else — to the nearby villages — so I can preach there also. That is why I have come." So he traveled throughout Galilee, preaching in their synagogues and driving out demons.*
>
> *Mark 1:35 – 39*

### Bible Discovery

### *Jesus Battles the Powers of Darkness*

We often think of Jesus as a wise, patient teacher. We readily imagine him reaching out to the poor, the outcasts, and the sick with love, mercy, healing, and hope. Although these images of Jesus are certainly true, we need to recognize that when it came to standing against evil, our compassionate Savior became a passionate warrior of righteousness. Jesus was not passive when it came to battling evil; he was fiercely confrontational.

1. Immediately after Jesus defeated the storm on the Sea of Galilee — the power of evil represented by the sea — who ran to meet him on the shore? (See Mark 4:35 - 5:13; Luke 8:22 - 33.)

How would you explain the underlying significance of these two events, and what do they reveal about Jesus?

What is the possible connection between these two events?

2. After Jesus cast the demons out of the man, they entered a herd of pigs and ran into the sea (Luke 8:30 – 33). What did the sea represent? (See Revelation 9:1 – 3, 11; 11:7; 17:8; 20:1 – 4.)

What were the demons acknowledging when they begged Jesus not to send them to the Abyss?

What, then, is the significance of the pigs rushing into the sea and drowning?

3. Jesus demonstrated his power over evil by casting out demons on many occasions. Read two of these accounts recorded in Mark 1:21 – 28 and Mark 9:14 – 29 and consider the following questions:

a. What does the demons' response to Jesus tell you about his power and the nature of the spiritual battle taking place in the world?

b. What demeanor did Jesus use in confronting the demons, and how did they respond?

c. How did the people respond when they saw what happened when Jesus confronted evil?

d. What difficulty did the disciples face in casting out the demon that possessed the boy? What was the solution?

4. In what ways did Jesus' teaching against evil and his active confrontation of it (demonstrated by healing the sick and casting out demons) affect people in his world? (See Matthew 4:23 – 25.)

What does Jesus' experience say to you about how we, as Christians, can make an impact in our world?

## DATA FILE

### Who Is Beelzebub?

- Baal-Zebul was the god of the Philistines and means "Exalted Baal" or "Prince Baal."
- The Hebrew name *Baal-Zebub* is a parody of Baal-Zebul and means "Lord of the Flies" (2 Kings 1:2–4).
- In the Greek language of the New Testament, the name becomes *Beelzebub*. Jesus used the name *Beelzebub* for Satan, the prince of demons. (See Matthew 10:25; 12:24–27; Mark 3:22; Luke 11:14–26.) This usage seems to indicate that Old Testament Baal worship was satanic—a tool Satan used to draw the Israelites away from God.

### What Is His Goal?

- First and foremost, Satan is the enemy of God's plan of salvation.
- He has devoted himself to destroying God's plan of salvation since the temptation of Adam and Eve in the garden of Eden (Genesis 3).
- He tried to use Herod to kill the baby Jesus (Matthew 2:13–18).
- He tempted Jesus at the beginning of his ministry, hoping that Jesus would compromise his mission (Matthew 4:1–11).

### How Did Jesus Confront Him?

While he was on earth, Jesus confronted Satan directly and had numerous confrontations with Satan's demons:

- He cast the demon out of the man in the synagogue (Mark 1:23–28).
- He cast a "legion" of demons out of the man of the tombs (Mark 5:1–20).
- He cast a demon out of a boy who couldn't speak and had seizures (Mark 9:14–29).
- He cast many demons out of people after he healed Peter's mother-in-law (Matthew 8:16).

## Reflection

Every day we each make a fundamental choice: to live as a disciple of Jesus, or not. We choose to obey his commands and seek his will or to live for ourselves. We choose to compromise with evil or to stand firm against it through the power of God. Imagine what might happen if every Christian were to follow the example of Jesus and love people enough to stand firmly against any form of evil!

When compared to the people of Jesus' day, many people in our culture seem to be less aware of the presence of evil in the world. Do you think Satan is any less active today than he was during the time Jesus ministered in Galilee? Why or why not?

In what ways do you think Satan might be disguising his work in order to avoid confrontation? List several examples.

In what ways do you think Satan is able to do his work freely because Christians overlook, fear, or ignore it and, therefore, don't confront him? Again, list specific examples.

What do you think is your role in standing against evil in your world? Be specific! Be honest!

How convinced are you of God's power over evil, and how has your belief influenced your view of evil and your willingness or ability to stand against it?

To strengthen your confidence in God's power over evil, you may want to list the ways in which Jesus defeated Satan, beginning with Jesus' ultimate victory: his death and resurrection.

## Memorize

*Jesus went throughout Galilee, teaching in their synagogues, preaching the good news of the kingdom, and healing every disease and sickness among the people. News about him spread all over Syria, and people brought to him all who were ill with various diseases, those suffering severe pain, the demon-possessed, those having seizures, and the paralyzed, and he healed them. Large crowds from Galilee, the Decapolis, Jerusalem, Judea and the region across the Jordan followed him.*

*Matthew 4:23 – 25*

## Day Two | From Spiritual Darkness into the Light

## The Very Words of God

*When Jesus spoke again to the people, he said, "I am the light of the world. Whoever follows me will never walk in darkness, but will have the light of life."*

*John 8:12*

## Bible Discovery

### *The Light Dawns for a Desperate Man*

Imagine how the disciples must have felt after Jesus stilled the storm that came up as they crossed the Sea of Galilee. The waves had swept over the boat, and the disciples had been terrified of drowning. Yet Jesus slept through the ordeal! Then, as soon as the boat reached the shore of the Decapolis, a demon-possessed man ran to greet them.

1. Describe the physical, emotional, and spiritual condition of the demon-possessed man who came to meet Jesus. In what way(s) might he have posed a threat to Jesus and his disciples? (See Mark 5:1 – 7; Luke 8:26 – 29.)

2. How did the man react to Jesus? Why? (See Mark 5:6 – 8; Luke 8:28.)

3. What was the name of the demons who possessed this man? (See Mark 5:9; Luke 8:30.)

   NOTE: This word may have a double meaning. It can, of course, mean a large number, but it could also be a representation of evil. A legion, which could have as many as six thousand Roman soldiers, was stationed at the Decapolis, and the symbol of that Roman legion was a boar's head. In Scripture, "Rome" sometimes symbolized evil and even the devil himself.

4.   After Jesus commanded the demons to leave the man, what immediate changes could people see? (See Mark 5:15; Luke 8:34 – 35.)

5.   Why do you think the local people reacted as they did to the healing of this man? (See Mark 5:17; Luke 8:35 – 37.)

## Reflection

Jesus did not avoid people who lived in spiritual darkness; he reached out to them. When the demon-possessed man came to him, Jesus, by the power and authority of God, dispelled the darkness of evil and brought about a lasting transformation in the man's life. If we are to bring God's light into our world, we need to recognize and reach out to people who live in darkness.

What are some of the ways in which the darkness of evil manifests itself in the lives of people in your world?

Clearly the demon-possessed man in this story was in miserable shape. The darkness of evil had its way with him. How do you respond to people in your world who obviously are being defeated by evil?

How do you think Jesus would respond to them? Why?

Other people who live in spiritual darkness seem as if they have it "all together." How do you respond to people in your world who appear to be in control of life, but serve Satan rather than God?

How do you think Jesus would respond to them? Why?

How willing are you to step out of your familiar, comfortable, and secure environment in order to interact with people who live in the darkness of evil and hold vastly different values and worldviews?

What specific things might God be calling you to do, in his power and authority, to pierce the darkness of sin in your world?

## DATA FILE

### The History of the Decapolis

Alexander the Great established a Greek presence in the Decapolis in 330 BC. In order to control the trade route from Arabia to Damascus and to protect the eastern frontier of the Roman Empire, the Roman general, Pompey, assumed control of the area and organized the region as a league of city-states in 64–63 BC. Although the Decapolis (derived from the Greek word *Decapolis*, meaning "ten cities") comprised more than ten city-states during much of its history, it retained its original name. During New Testament times, the pagan cities in the Decapolis, which was located to the south and east of the Sea of Galilee, remained a league of free city-states under the umbrella of Roman authority.

### The Glory of the Decapolis

Today, the ruins of the Decapolis district still provide evidence of its ancient Greek splendor and Hellenistic culture:

- A fifteen-mile-long aqueduct brought water to Susita, a city built on a thirty-five-acre plateau. One of the more modern Hellenistic cities of the Decapolis, Susita boasted pagan temples, magnificent examples of Greek architecture, paved streets, and fountains.
- In other Decapolis cities, temples honored local gods and glorified the excesses of pleasure.
- The beautiful bath complex at Hammat Gader, located about five miles from the Sea of Galilee, made use of hot mineral springs from the nearby Gilead Mountains. At least eight pools—including one more than a hundred feet long that featured thirty-two marble fountains—soothed bathers. Some visitors no doubt came to the region to find healing in the warm baths (there was even a separate pool for lepers) and to worship the gods of healing.
- Colonnaded streets, running water, and marble fountains were common in the cities of the Decapolis, as were such buildings as theaters, stadiums, and temples that represented Greek ideals.

## The Culture of the Decapolis

The cities of the Decapolis were fully immersed in Greek culture. Hellenism—the humanistic religion of the Greeks—glorified sexuality, the human form, and the excesses of pleasure, violence, and wealth. It preached that truth could be known only through the human mind and that pleasure was a crucial goal in life. Daily life in the Decapolis included festivals that celebrated pagan holidays and theaters that portrayed erotic themes.

Although the religious Jews of Jesus' day opposed the values and practices of Hellenism, the Greek educational system of the region had instilled Greek ideas into generations of young Jewish people. Young Jews read Greek mythology and philosophy and learned to draw and sculpt the forms of Greek gods. The Pharisees, who were devoted to keeping God's people faithful to Torah, constantly admonished young Jews who were intrigued by Greek culture.

## Hope for the Decapolis

Jesus deliberately brought the gospel to the people in this region because they needed the healing of body and soul that God alone could provide. The pagan gods and ideals of Hellenism provided only a false hope.

- After Jesus met a demon-possessed man and drove out his demons, the man told the inhabitants of a nearby city (probably Susita) what had happened to him (Mark 5:1–20). Perhaps as a result of seeing the demon-possessed man healed and in his right mind, a number of people became Christians, making the city a center of early Christianity. Remains of at least five large churches have been found in Susita.
- When people found no cure in the baths at Hammat Gader, some of them turned to Jesus, whose healing powers were known in the Decapolis (Mark 7:31–37). Even though the culture of the Decapolis was sophisticated and promoted "healing," the people needed Jesus' healing power most of all.

# Day Three | The Power of One

### The Very Words of God

> *"Go home to your family and tell them how much the Lord has done for you, and how he has had mercy on you." So the man went away and began to tell in the Decapolis how much Jesus had done for him. And all the people were amazed.*
>
> Mark 5:19–20

### Bible Discovery

### *One Changed Man Tells His Story*

We don't know exactly what the man who had been demon-possessed said, and we don't know how he said it, but we do know that news of the miracle God had done for him spread throughout the Decapolis. His life illustrates how God can use any of us, no matter our background, training, or experience, to spiritually impact our communities and penetrate the darkest strongholds of evil.

1.  What kind of a response did Jesus and his disciples receive when they revisited the Decapolis some time after he had healed the demon-possessed man? (See Matthew 15:29–31; Mark 7:31–37.)



    What do you think accounted for this dramatic difference?



2.  How had the people in the Decapolis heard about Jesus? (See Mark 5:18–20; Luke 8:38–39.)

What, according to this biblical story, is the key to evangelism?

What seems unusual or surprising to you about the way in which God used this one man to establish a strong Christian community in a pagan culture?

What do you learn from the spiritual impact of one formerly demon-possessed man who knew no theology yet became an effective missionary in this most pagan area of first-century Israel?

## Reflection

If you are a Christian who obeys God, he desires to use you to reflect his love and truth, no matter how tough the mission field may be. Sometimes that can be as simple as sharing what Jesus has done for you with people you meet in everyday life. It isn't necessary for us to have a wealth of knowledge or special training before we can make a positive impact in our communities. God can use us just the way we are.

What has the story of the demon-possessed man shown you about the impact one person can have if he or she has a grateful heart and a desire to serve God?

Witnessing is simply sharing with people you meet in everyday life about what Jesus has done. How might remembering that basic truth encourage you to witness more often?

What is your story? How has what Jesus accomplished through his death and resurrection changed your life?

Who knows about it?

With whom might God want you to share what he has done for you?

What may be keeping you from sharing your story?

## Memorize

*How, then, can they call on the one they have not believed in? And how can they believe in the one of whom they have not heard? And how can they hear without someone preaching to them? And how can they preach unless they are sent? As it is written, "How beautiful are the feet of those who bring good news!"*

*Romans 10:14–15*

# Day Four | Old Testament Heroes Who Confronted Evil

## The Very Words of God

*Just as he had done at Bethel, Josiah removed and defiled all the shrines at the high places that the kings of Israel had built in the towns of Samaria that had provoked the LORD to anger.... Josiah got rid of the mediums and spiritists, the household gods, the idols and all the other detestable things seen in Judah and Jerusalem. This he did to fulfill the requirements of the law written in the book that Hilkiah the priest had discovered in the temple of the LORD. Neither before nor after Josiah was there a king like him who turned to the LORD as he did — with all his heart and with all his soul and with all his strength, in accordance with all the Law of Moses.*

*2 Kings 23:19, 24 – 25*

## Bible Discovery

### Standing Firm for God

Jesus is not the only person mentioned in the Bible who went out of his way to confront evil. The Old Testament texts tell the stories of many of God's people who chose to stand for God. They boldly faced the forces of darkness and displayed the power of God for all to see. Although we may never face hundreds of pagan prophets or a whole nation that has turned its back on God, we are still called to stand strong in the battle against evil. As you read about the following people who stood up for God, think about your life and what God would have you do to confront evil.

1. Elijah (See 1 Kings 18:16 – 40.)

   a. What evil did Elijah confront? What did he say to King Ahab and the Israelites? (See 1 Kings 18:16 – 21.)

b. What "test" did Elijah propose? (See 1 Kings 18:22 – 25.)

c. What was the result? (See 1 Kings 18:26 – 40.)

2. David (See 1 Samuel 17.)

a. Who did Satan use to defy Israel and their God? (See 1 Samuel 17:4 – 10.)

b. Who battled the giant? Why? By whose power was the giant killed? (See 1 Samuel 17:32 – 37, 45 – 50.)

3. Phineas (See Numbers 25:1 – 13.)

a. What were the Israelites doing that was evil in the sight of God? (See Numbers 25:1 – 3.)

b. What strong measures did God order to confront this evil? (See Numbers 25:4 – 5.)

c. What did Phineas do? What was the result? (See Numbers 25:6 – 9.)

4. Josiah (See 2 Kings 23:1 – 25.)

   a. What did King Josiah do first, before he confronted the evil in Judah? Why was this important? (See 2 Kings 23:1 – 3.)

   b. Which radical actions did Josiah take to confront evil? Why were these necessary? (See 2 Kings 23:4 – 16, 19 – 20.)

   c. What celebration did Josiah reinstitute? (See 2 Kings 23:21 – 23.)

   d. What kind of commitment is required to challenge evil effectively at its core? (See 2 Chronicles 34:29 – 33; 2 Kings 23:25.)

   NOTE: Other examples of Old Testament people who confronted evil include Deborah (Judges 4) and Esther (Esther 3:8 – 11; 4:1 – 17; 5:1 – 8; 7:1 – 10).

## Reflection

God's people have always been called to stand with him in the battle against Satan and all that is evil in the world. But the task is not easy (it takes courage and conviction), and those who commit to it are often unpopular. The question that every Christian today must ask is, "Am I responding to God's battle call? Am I fully committed to keeping God's commands with all my heart, soul, and strength?"

As you think about the examples you just read of godly people who confronted evil in ancient times, what did you learn that applies to your life and walk with God? Use the chart below and on page 71 to help you begin that process.

| The example of God's ancient warriors against evil | Me, as God's warrior against evil |
|---|---|
| How did they become aware of the evil God wanted them to confront? | What changes might I need to make in my lifestyle so that I will be more aware of God's perspective on evil and how he wants to defeat it? |
| How were they equipped for the battle God called them to fight? | How has God prepared me to stand with him against evil, and to what extent do I trust him to provide whatever I need to accomplish what he calls me to do? |

| What would have happened if they had not chosen to act against evil? | What might be the consequences if I do not act against evil? |
|---|---|
| What risks did they face, and what personal price were they willing to pay in order to obey God? | What risk am I willing to face, and what price am I willing to pay in order to be God's warrior against evil? |

## Memorize

*Therefore, my dear brothers, stand firm. Let nothing move you. Always give yourselves fully to the work of the Lord, because you know that your labor in the Lord is not in vain.*

*1 Corinthians 15:58*

# Day Five | A Call to Action

## The Very Words of God

> *What good is it, my brothers, if a man claims to have faith but has no deeds? Can such faith save him? Suppose a brother or sister is without clothes and daily food. If one of you says to him, "Go, I wish you well; keep warm and well fed," but does nothing about his physical needs, what good is it?*
>
> James 2:14–16

## Bible Discovery

### Choose to Confront Personal Evil

Throughout Scripture, God calls Christians to respond compassionately and appropriately to such personal evil as injustice, hatred, hunger, and oppression. Jesus demonstrated uncommon love and concern for the outcasts, the weak, the unloved, and the despised people of his day. His example is a testimony to how much God cares about people who are deeply affected by personal evil. His example is a constant reminder of how we must step out of our secure environment to confront evil in the power and name of Jesus.

1. How does God view issues of justice? (See Leviticus 19:15; Deuteronomy 27:19; Psalms 11:7; 103:6.)

   What perspective do these Scripture texts give you on places in your culture where God might want you to confront evil?

2.  What did the prophet Isaiah urge God's people to do? (See Isaiah 1:17.)



    In which practical ways can you do this in your world? What specific things can you do to pierce the darkness of evil in these situations?



3.  When we live in a fast-paced, self-gratifying culture, it is easy for us to become self-serving or calloused and ignore the impact of evil on weak, vulnerable people. But God never overlooks or ignores those who are oppressed by evil.

    a.  What promise does God make in Exodus 22:22 – 24, and what impact does it have on how quickly you reach out to those who are oppressed by evil?



    b.  What strong criticism did Jesus give to the Pharisees in Matthew 23:23, and what impact does it have on how you live your life?



4.  What do you learn from the following examples of how Jesus confronted evil and demonstrated his love to "outsiders" and vulnerable people? (See Matthew 8:2 – 3; Luke 7:12 – 15; John 8:3 – 11.)

5. If we are to be effective in taking a stand against evil, how important is it that our faith be linked to our outward actions? (See James 2:2 – 3, 14 – 16.)

## Reflection

Ezekiel 18:7 – 9 paints a broad picture of what it means to live a righteous life — to stand for God and confront what is evil as a natural part of everyday life. God calls each of us to give ourselves fully to him and make a difference in our world by piercing the darkness with his light. So take time to read this text and pray about its practical meaning. Make the commitment to examine the attitudes of your heart and discover what action God would have you take in order to confront personal evil in your community.

> *He does not oppress anyone,*
> > *but returns what he took in pledge for a loan.*
> *He does not commit robbery*
> > *but gives his food to the hungry*
> > *and provides clothing for the naked.*
> *He does not lend at usury*
> > *or take excessive interest.*
> *He withholds his hand from doing wrong*
> > *and judges fairly between man and man.*
> *He follows my decrees*
> > *and faithfully keeps my laws.*
> *That man is righteous;*
> > *he will surely live, declares the Sovereign* LORD.

# GATES OF HADES (HELL)

Shortly before his crucifixion, Jesus took his disciples to Caesarea Philippi, a pagan city located in the northeastern part of Israel at the foot of Mount Hermon, Israel's highest mountain. Built by Herod Philip, who was a son of Herod the Great, Caesarea Philippi was about twenty-five miles away from the area of Galilee in which Jesus focused his ministry. For many years, during Old Testament times, people in the region that later included Caesarea Philippi had worshiped false gods, including Baal (Joshua 11:16 – 17; 12:7). Just a few miles away, in the city of Dan, King Jeroboam had set up the golden calf on a "high place" (1 Kings 12:25 – 31). During Jesus' time, the people in this region worshiped the Greek fertility gods.

The ancient name of Caesarea Philippi was Panias — named after "Pan," the fertility god of mountains and forests, who was one of the gods worshiped at this stunningly beautiful site. One of three springs that feed the Jordan River flows out from the base of a cliff that is more than one hundred feet high. During the time of Jesus, the spring gushed from a cave, which has since collapsed. Ancient people believed that gods entered the underworld through caves and that Baal caused the dry season each year by entering caves such as this one, which would have been known as a "gate of Hades." The cliff could also be referred to as the "Rock of the Gods" because people built temples and shrines at the base of the cliff and cut openings into the rock face above, in which they placed idols and statues of gods and goddesses.

It may surprise us that Jesus deliberately led his disciples on a two-day walk over mountainous terrain in order to teach them at this thriving center of pagan religion. Yet this was where he chose to give his disciples their "graduation talk." This is where he taught them a profound lesson about his purpose and the mission to which he had called them. In this setting, Jesus asked his disciples, "Who do people say the Son of Man is?" After listening to their answers, he asked the more important question: "Who do you say I am?"

Peter, who may have been standing near the pagan shrines, stated, "You are the Christ, the Son of the living God."

Jesus then said, "You are Peter, and on this rock I will build my church, and the gates of Hades [hell] will not overcome it."

Different traditions emphasize different aspects of this statement. Catholic tradition emphasizes that the church is built on Peter and his work. Protestant tradition emphasizes that Peter's confession is the rock on which the church is built. But in the powerful setting of this ancient shrine, Jesus may also have intended to communicate a symbolic meaning: that his church would be built on the pagan "rock" — the rock into which idols had been placed, the rock on which the golden calf had been placed, the rock that represented pagan worship and ungodly values. In effect, Jesus was saying that his church would replace the very power and strength of the devil!

Jesus also said that "the gates of Hades" [hell] would not prove stronger than his church. Because gates are designed to keep out enemies, Jesus was saying that if his church remained rooted in him — the Messiah — and his methods remained its methods, it would overcome even the gates of hell. So, like Jesus' disciples, who after three years of preparation were ready to "graduate" and begin their ministry, we Christians today are to prepare ourselves to confront the gates of hell — the devil's strength and power. In Jesus' power, those gates will fall.

## Opening Thoughts (4 minutes)

*The Very Words of God*

> *Then Jesus said to his disciples, "If anyone would come after me, he must deny himself and take up his cross and follow me. For whoever wants to save his life will lose it, but whoever loses his life for me will find it. What good will it be for a man if he gains the whole world, yet forfeits his soul? Or what can a man give in exchange for his soul?*
>
> *Matthew 16:24 – 26*

### Think About It

Think for a moment about how Christians today view the church and the ways in which it impacts culture.

Would you say the church is on the offensive against evil, or has it taken a defensive position? Explain your answer and how you think it influences the ability of the church and the Christian community to impact culture for Christ.

## DVD Teaching Notes (19 minutes)

### Pagan influence in Caesarea Philippi

### Jesus' message to his disciples

### The mission of the church

## DVD Discussion (7 minutes)

On the map below note how far Caesarea Philippi was from Capernaum and the Sea of Galilee. Note also Mount Hermon, the beginnings of the Jordan River, and the city of Dan.

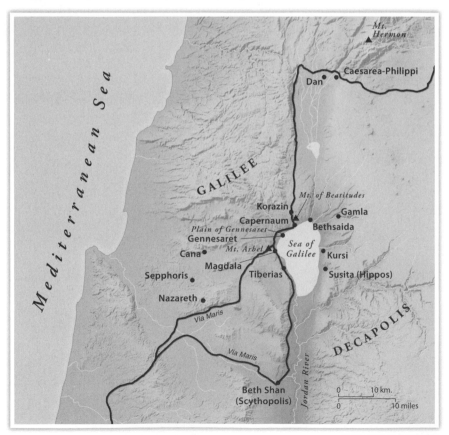

**SEA OF GALILEE**

1.  What do you think the disciples might have been thinking
    as they traveled with Jesus to Caesarea Philippi — on the way
    there *and* on the way back?

2.  Which images in this video — the flowing water, the cave,
    the "rock of the gods," the "gates of Hades" — made the
    greatest impact on you and your understanding of Jesus and
    his message? Why?

3.  How does the perspective that the church is to take the
    offensive rather than the defensive against evil, as repre-
    sented by the "gates of Hades," affect your view of ministry?
    How do you think it affected the disciples' view?

## IDENTITY PROFILE
### Who Was Baal?

- The fertility god of the Canaanites.
- Considered to be the supreme god because he had defeated the sea god and so controlled the sea and could prevent storms.
- Believed to have power over weather.
- Often depicted as a man with the head and horns of a bull, carrying a lightning bolt in his hand(s).
- Attractive to his followers because of his supposed ability to provide rain in a dry country.
- Supposedly went to the land of the dead, the underworld, each year and returned to bring rain to the earth and create abundant harvests.
- Was appeased through sacrifices, usually animals (1 Kings 18:23), although during times of crisis Baal's followers sometimes sacrificed their children (Deuteronomy 12:31; 18:9–11).
- Thought to have a mistress, Asherah — the fertility goddess. Believing that the sexual union of Baal and Asherah produced fertility, pagan worshipers engaged in immoral sex to entice the gods to join together and ensure good harvests.

## Small Group Bible Discovery and Discussion (19 minutes)

*Our Hope Is in the Living God!*

When the Israelites entered the Promised Land, they found a land of farmers who attributed its fertility to their god, Baal. The Israelites experienced their God in the desert and were easily enticed by the fertility gods of Canaan. They sometimes worshiped the God who had guided them to the Promised Land, sometimes worshiped the fertility gods, and sometimes worshiped both. As was true in ancient times, God's people still face the same choice: will we be totally committed to the one true, living God or will we place our trust in the dead "gods" of the places we inhabit?

1.  What is the difference between the living God and idols such as Pan, the fertility god worshiped in Caesarea Philippi? (See Jeremiah 10:1 – 16.)

2.  In the following passages, note the ways in which the living God of Israel demonstrated his supremacy over Baal, the dead god of the Canaanites.

| Scripture Text | God's Power Demonstrated |
|---|---|
| Josh. 3:9–17 | |
| Judg. 5:19–21 | |
| 1 Kings 17:1; 18:1, 21–45 | |
| 2 Kings 2:8, 11–14, 19–22 | |

## DID YOU KNOW?

Water played a focal role in many confrontations between God and his people and Baal and the Canaanite people. Why? Perhaps it had to do with how ancient people viewed their natural world in relationship to their gods. For example, in the minds of ancient people, to have life you must have water. Life comes from god, so where there is water, there must be god. So when God stopped the Jordan River, withheld rain, or caused floods, it was more than a demonstration of his control over nature; it was an attack on the heart of pagan beliefs because it showed that his power was greater than that of the pagan gods.

3. After God led them into the Promised Land, what did the Israelites do? (See Judges 2:10 – 13.)

   How did God respond to them, and how do you think he responds to us when we abandon our commitment to the living God?

4. What are some of the dead "gods" that people in our culture worship, and in what ways do these gods contrast with the true, living God?

5. In what ways do you see the community of Christians simply coexisting with, rather than confronting, the gods of this world?

   What message(s) about the living God do we send to people around us when we don't stand against the gods of this world?

# Faith Lesson (5 minutes)

In Matthew 16, Jesus asked his disciples who people said he was, then he asked his disciples who they recognized him to be. Peter answered, "You are the Christ, the Son of the living God." How we answer Jesus' question today dramatically influences how we respond to him and the evil "gods" of our world.

1.  Have you come to the point in your life when you, like Peter, have stated with conviction, "You are the Christ, the Son of the living God"?

    If yes, what impact does this belief have on your life, and in what ways should it have more of an impact? If no, who do you believe Jesus is, and in what ways does this belief impact your life?

2.  Second Corinthians 4:4 says that Satan has blinded the minds of unbelievers so that they cannot see Christ. What do you see Satan doing today to keep people focused on false "gods" rather than on Jesus the Messiah?

    What is it about wealth, physical beauty, intellect, power, thrill-seeking, fame, youth, security, luxurious living, sexual pleasure, and the like that is so enticing and makes it difficult for us to recognize when such things become gods?

What can and are you doing to help open the eyes of people who are focused on these things so that they will see and come to place their hope in the living God?

3. Do you know people who are effectively confronting the "gods" and evil of this world? If so, what can you learn from them that will help you to reveal the living God to others?

## Closing (1 minute)

Read together 1 Timothy 4:9: "This is a trustworthy saying that deserves full acceptance (and for this we labor and strive), that we have put our hope in the living God, who is the Savior of all men, and especially of those who believe." Then pray, asking God for confidence and courage in confronting Satan and the "dead gods" of this age. Confess any desires to pursue the gods of this world and pray for increased faithfulness and wisdom in living for God and his values. Thank him that he is the living God who is worthy of all honor, praise, and glory.

### Memorize

*This is a trustworthy saying that deserves full acceptance (and for this we labor and strive), that we have put our hope in the living God, who is the Savior of all men, and especially of those who believe.*

**1 Timothy 4:9**

# When Following Jesus Is the Most Important Thing in Life

*In-Depth Personal Study Sessions*

## Day One | Israel Steps into Idolatry

### The Very Words of God

> *After seeking advice, the king [Jeroboam] made two golden calves. He said to the people, "It is too much for you to go up to Jerusalem. Here are your gods, O Israel, who brought you up out of Egypt." One he set up in Bethel, and the other in Dan. And this thing became a sin; the people went even as far as Dan to worship the one there.*
>
> *1 Kings 12:28 – 30*

### Bible Discovery

### The Religious History of Northern Israel

Certain places in the ancient Near East were considered to be sacred and, because of its natural springs and history as a pagan worship center, Caesarea Philippi was one of them. Tragically, the tribe of Dan had a role in establishing this area of northern Israel as a center for pagan worship. Despite all that the living God of Israel had done for his people, the tribe of Dan rejected the land God had given them. They chose their own homeland and their own gods, the dead gods of Canaan. Then, when Jeroboam became king of Israel (the northern kingdom), he established a pagan worship center featuring a golden calf at Dan, and idolatry became deeply rooted in Israel.

1. What did the tribe of Dan do with their God-given inheritance of land in Canaan? (See Joshua 19:40 – 47.)

2. How did God respond to their disobedience? (See Judges 2:1 – 3.)

3. How did the Danites acquire their idols and their land? (See Judges 18:1 – 2, 11 – 20, 27 – 31.)

   Although they still retained some forms of the worship practices of Israel, what indications do you see that worshiping God and obeying his commands was becoming less important to them?

4. After Solomon's death, Israel split into two kingdoms. Realizing that the temple of Jerusalem was now in Judah (southern kingdom) under King Rehoboam's control, what steps did King Jeroboam of Israel (northern kingdom) take to firmly establish idol worship as the religion of his kingdom? (See 1 Kings 12:26 – 33.)

5. For generations, most of the kings of Israel followed in the steps of King Jeroboam. What impact did the idolatry of Israel's kings have on all of Israel, Judah, the surrounding regions, and the testimony of the living God in the world? (See 2 Kings 17:6 – 8, 13 – 23.)

Considering that God wanted the tribe of Dan to defeat the pagan gods and possess the land for the glory of the living God, how important do you think it is for us to obey God and confront the gods of our culture? In what specific ways might we do this?

## Reflection

The pagan worship centers of northern Israel, some of which were in place during the time of the judges, were still being used during New Testament times. At Caesarea Philippi, worship of the Roman and Greek gods had replaced the worship of Baal, but the worship practices were similar. Clearly the choices of the ancient Israelites to turn away from following the living God had a devastating and long-lasting impact.

In what ways do you think the Danites' failure to follow God's assignment for them (to possess the land he had given them) was related to their idol worship?

What do you learn from the saga of Israel's idol worship about the responsibility of Christians today to defeat evil and reclaim the world for God?

What can *you* do?

How does Satan use even the "smallest" sins to trap us — and affect generations to come?

With this in mind, which sin(s) do you continue to commit, knowing full well that it is damaging your relationship with God?

How willing are you to start, right now, to repent of your sin and pursue the path of righteousness God has provided?

## Day Two | Jesus the Messiah, Son of the Living God

### The Very Words of God

> *Andrew, Simon Peter's brother, was one of the two who heard what John had said and who had followed Jesus. The first thing Andrew did was to find his brother Simon and tell him, "We have found the Messiah" (that is, the Christ). And he brought him to Jesus.*
>
> John 1:40 – 42

### Bible Discovery

### *Understanding Who the Messiah Was and Why He Came*

Jesus came to earth to fulfill the Scriptures, to proclaim the news of the kingdom of God, and to defeat Satan by suffering, dying, and being raised from the dead. Because he knew where this journey would lead him, and ultimately lead his early disciples as well, he knew how important it was for them to believe that he was, indeed, the long-awaited Messiah.

1.  Which roles, according to Deuteronomy 18:18 and Zechariah 6:12 – 13, would the Messiah fulfill?

2.  Who did the people recognize Jesus to be? (See Matthew 21:10 – 11.)

3.  How did God publicly affirm that Jesus was equipped and given God's authority to fulfill his role as Messiah? (See Matthew 3:16 – 17.)

4.  After Jesus asked his disciples who other people thought he was, what did he ask them? (See Matthew 16:15 – 16; Mark 8:29.)

    Why was it important for the disciples to be able to answer this question correctly?

    In light of where Jesus and his disciples were (a place where people worshiped the "dead" gods of pagan religions), what is significant about the words Peter used in his response to Jesus?

## DATA FILE
### Jesus Christ the Messiah

As English-speaking Christians, we refer to our Savior as *Jesus Christ* and *Messiah.* There is great richness of meaning behind these three words.

- *Jesus* is the English form of the name found in Greek versions of the New Testament. The Hebrew name translated *Jesus* was *Yeshua*, a shortened version of the word *Y'hoshua,* which means "Yahweh saves," and in English is translated Joshua.
- *Christ* is the English translation of the Greek word *Christos*, which means "Messiah." Therefore the words *Messiah* and *Christ* are the same, although *Messiah* better reflects the Jewish setting of Jesus' ministry.
- *Messiah* means "anointed" and is rooted in the Old Testament. It refers to the pouring (anointing) of oil on people who were marked by God as uniquely qualified for a task or office. This anointing was a symbol of the authority a person received from God. (That's why Jesus' baptism is so significant — Matthew 3:13 – 17.) Every anointed person (e.g., prophet, priest, and king) was, in the sense of having been anointed, *a* messiah. The prophets predicted that one day God would send his deliverer — "the ultimate Messiah" — who would combine the roles of prophet, priest, and king. However, the people of Jesus' day emphasized the kingly role of Messiah, whom they believed would use military force to deliver them from the political oppression of Rome.

## Reflection

Jesus, the Son of the living God, came to earth to be the Savior of the world. He was widely known as a teacher, a rabbi. He was a king, but his kingdom was not of this world. Most important, he was the Lamb of God who would pour out his blood as a sacrifice for the sins of all humanity. But it was hard for people, even for his disciples, to accept this aspect of his mission as the Messiah.

What if Jesus had been the king many people expected him to be? What if he had overcome Israel's Roman oppressors?

How might our world and our lives be different today if Jesus had been king but not Savior?

How important are our beliefs about Jesus' identity, and in what ways do they affect how we live?

Who do people today say that Jesus was — or is?

In what ways do their answers differ from yours?

What do you find is the most difficult truth for people to accept about Jesus?

What has been your experience with professing Jesus as Messiah, Son of the living God, to people who believe something different about him?

What have you found to be the most effective way to share your conviction of Jesus' identity with those who see him as someone else?

## Memorize

*For us there is but one God, the Father, from whom all things came and for whom we live; and there is but one Lord, Jesus Christ, through whom all things came and through whom we live.*

**1 Corinthians 8:6**

## Day Three | The Victory of Our Suffering Messiah

### The Very Words of God

*Jesus said to her, "I am the resurrection and the life. He who believes in me will live, even though he dies; and whoever lives and believes in me will never die. Do you believe this?" "Yes, Lord," she told him, "I believe that you are the Christ, the Son of God, who was to come into the world."*

**John 11:25–27**

### Bible Discovery

### *Jesus Gave Us Life by Triumphing over Death*

At Caesarea Philippi, Jesus taught his disciples one of his most profound and difficult lessons. In a way, it was the climax of his teaching ministry. From Caesarea Philippi, Jesus set his heart toward Jerusalem, where he would die. Great suffering and sacrifice lay ahead — for him and for the disciples he loved. He came to challenge Satan by suffering and dying; then he triumphed over death — the "gates of Hades" — through his bodily resurrection from the grave. Because of who he is and what he suffered, anyone who believes in him will receive eternal life.

1. No sooner had Peter made his profession of faith than Jesus began to prepare his disciples for the unthinkable.

   a. What shocking news did Jesus need to tell them, and why do you think he chose this moment to begin revealing it? (See Matthew 16:21 – 26; Mark 8:31.)

   b. What kind of life did Isaiah the prophet say that Jesus would have, and to what extent do you think the disciples envisioned this actually happening to Jesus? (See Isaiah 53:1 – 12.)

   c. In light of John 6:14 – 15, why do you think it was so difficult for the people of Jesus' day, including his disciples, to understand what he — the Messiah — was called to do?

2. As Christians, why are we no longer "slaves to sin"? (See John 3:16 – 17; Romans 6:8 – 14.)

3. What promise and hope do we have because Jesus was willing to suffer, die, and rise from the dead? (See 1 Corinthians 15:20 – 26; 1 Peter 1:3 – 4.)

## THE TRUTH OF THE MATTER

To believe in Jesus (*Yeshua*) is to accept his work of saving sinners from sin and to accept the mission to take on the "gates of hell." To believe in Christ (Messiah, *Mashiach*) is to confess that he was chosen and equipped by God for his office as prophet, priest, and king. Jesus accomplished the task he was sent to do by serving others and suffering for them, even unto death. Following Christ means accepting his command to suffer for him and to serve others on his behalf. When we engage in the process of believing and following, we are truly Christian (Christlike).

## Reflection

Here on earth, we must deal with all kinds of evil. Relationships are broken. Injustice is rampant. Christians are persecuted in various countries. But because of the sacrifice of Jesus and his victory over death, every Christian can look forward to an amazing eternity in heaven.

Why is Jesus' resurrection such an important truth of Christianity?

How do you think it motivated his early disciples to keep preaching about it despite great persecution?

If you truly believe that one day you will live with the resurrected Christ, what difference should that make in your everyday life?

When you suffer from face-to-face encounters with evil in your life, in your relationships with others, or as you fight against the impact of evil in the world, what hope do you find in the truth of Jesus' resurrection — and the future resurrection of all Christians?

## Memorize

*Praise be to the God and Father of our Lord Jesus Christ! In his great mercy he has given us new birth into a living hope through the resurrection of Jesus Christ from the dead, and into an inheritance that can never perish, spoil or fade — kept in heaven for you.*

*1 Peter 1:3 – 4*

## Day Four | The Meaning of the "Rock"

## The Very Words of God

*And I tell you that you are Peter, and on this rock I will build my church, and the gates of Hades will not overcome it.*

*Matthew 16:18*

## Bible Discovery

### Building on the "Rock"

Imagine following Jesus for two days over hillsides and rocky terrain to get to Caesarea Philippi, a location famous for its pagan rituals and sacrifices. Here, at the base of a great cliff, people once believed that gods such as Baal entered a cave, the "gates of Hades," that led to the underworld. Here, frenzied people committed sexual immorality in the hopes of receiving great harvests. And here, at a focal point of pagan religion, Jesus prepared his disciples for their future ministry in pagan lands. Built on the "rock," the early church would be at the center of God's powerful work in confronting evil.

1.  On what did Jesus promise to build his church? (See Matthew 16:18.)



    What do you think is the significance of Jesus' description, "*this* rock?"




2.  There are two major viewpoints concerning what Jesus meant by the "rock" on which he would build his church. What does the Bible say about:

    a.  Peter — representing all the disciples — being the "rock"? (See Ephesians 2:20 – 21.)



    b.  Peter's profession — that Jesus is the Christ, the Son of the living God — being the "rock"? (See Acts 4:10 – 11; 1 Corinthians 3:10 – 15.)



3.  The imagery of the "rock" was not new to the disciples, who were familiar with the Scriptures.

    a.  On which "rock" was the nation of Israel built? (See Isaiah 51:1 – 2.)

b. In Psalm 18:2 – 3, who is the "rock" whom David praised, and to what did he liken it?

c. Who did David choose to be his "rock"? (See Psalm 62:5 – 7.)

## Reflection

Today, those of us who are Christians face challenges similar to those faced by the early disciples who stood with Jesus in Caesarea Philippi. Although we are not standing next to a cliff face covered with pagan idols and shrines, we live in a culture that has rooted itself in the "rock" of many other idols of evil. Our calling is to stand against that evil in the power of Jesus, the Messiah, Son of the living God.

On which man-made "rocks" do people today build their hopes and their lives? Make a list of them!

What effect does dependence on idols of evil have on those who worship them, particularly on their view of God and their relationship with him?

What is the impact on their loved ones? On their communities? On their culture?

In which specific ways might God be calling you to use the power of his redemption against these examples of evil?

Why is it essential that we depend on God to be our "rock" when we stand against the evil in our culture?

What confidence do you have that you can depend on God's power to confront even the places in society where Satan is strongest — the places where ungodly beliefs are boldly practiced and promoted?

Jesus said, "Everyone who hears these words of mine and puts them into practice is like a wise man who built his house on the rock" (Matthew 7:24). What are you doing to remain firmly rooted on the "rock" of his words?

## **Day Five** | Christ's Church — On the Offensive Against Evil

### The Very Words of God

*Do not be afraid. I am the First and the Last. I am the Living One; I was dead, and behold I am alive for ever and ever! And I hold the keys of death and Hades.*

*Revelation 1:17 – 18*

### Bible Discovery

### *Confronting the Gates of Hades (Hell)*

Hades — originally the Greek god of the underworld — is the namesake for the place where departed spirits live. It is frequently used in the Bible as a synonym for hell or the grave. Based on the way in which Jesus used it in Matthew 16:18, Hades seems to refer to the powers of evil that resisted Jesus, including Satan's ultimate weapon — physical death. As Jesus began to teach his disciples their future mission and the mission of his church, he made a powerful statement: the gates of hell itself could not stand against it!

1.  What did Jesus say his church would have to confront, and what would be the outcome? (See Matthew 16:18.)

2.  How can we be assured of this outcome? (See 1 John 3:7 – 8; 4:2 – 4.)

3. What was Jesus' method of defeating Satan, sin, and physical death — the "gates of Hades"? (See Matthew 16:21 – 23; 1 Corinthians 15:26 – 28.)

4. Jesus has given an enormous challenge to his church, but he has also empowered the church to confront evil. Read the following Scripture passages and begin compiling a list of the power and hope Jesus has given to the church to accomplish its task.

| Scripture Text | The Power and Hope of the Church |
|---|---|
| Luke 10:17 – 20 | |
| Acts 1:8 | |
| Eph. 1:17 – 23 | |
| Eph. 6:10 – 18 | |
| Heb. 4:12 – 16 | |

## Reflection

Although the pagan values around us may appear to be dominant, Jesus has promised that the "gates of Hades" will not win. The evil realm of Satan is already on the defensive against the church of Jesus. So the mission of the people of God is to take on evil. Wherever we see what isn't God's way, we need to take it on!

What are some ways in which your local church is battling evil in Jesus' name?

Would you say that the activities of your local faith community are primarily defensive or offensive when it comes to opposing evil? Why?

How do you think the fear many Christians have about confronting the "gates of Hades" has damaged the church — its body, its influence, its reputation, its outreach?

Why must your church be on the front lines of the battle against evil in your community?

Where do you encounter the "gates of Hades" in your life?

What are you doing personally to challenge that evil in the name of Jesus?

What will you commit to do as a result of what you have learned in this session?

I will prepare myself and actively use _____ _____ (the gifts, abilities, and opportunities God has given me) to challenge _____ (the evil within my sphere of influence) in the name and power of Jesus. Amen.

## Memorize

*For though we live in the world, we do not wage war as the world does. The weapons we fight with are not the weapons of the world. On the contrary, they have divine power to demolish strongholds.*

*2 Corinthians 10:3 – 4*

# CITY OF THE GREAT KING — THE TEMPLE

To walk down the streets of Jerusalem is to walk where history was unfolding more than a thousand years before Jesus came to earth. Jerusalem is where pivotal events in both Judaism and Christianity have taken place. As we better understand that city's history, we gain insights into the land and people of ancient Israel. Even more important, we gain a richer understanding of the great work of redemption God accomplished there.

The story of Jerusalem begins in approximately 2000 BC when God commanded Abraham to offer a sacrifice to him in the region of Mount Moriah, a high plateau in the Judea Mountains. Later, David captured the ancient Canaanite city of Jebus that had been built on Mount Moriah (1 Chronicles 11:4 - 5). He renamed it the City of David and thus established the religious and political capital of the people and nation of Israel that became known as Jerusalem.

In obedience to God's leading, David selected the site for God's temple, which his son, Solomon, built in about 950 BC. Solomon's temple was eventually destroyed, but King Herod rebuilt and greatly expanded the Temple Mount. Jesus worshiped, learned, and taught in that temple. And just outside its walls, Jesus committed the greatest act of love and redemption the world will ever know. After his resurrection, disciples of Jesus who were empowered by the Spirit given to them at Pentecost spread the Christian faith from the temple in Jerusalem to the uttermost ends of the earth.

In this video, with the help of a large-scale model of what the temple and city of Jerusalem looked like during Jesus' time, you'll learn about God's temple. Because the temple was the dwelling place of God, the place God chose to bear his name and house his presence on earth, it was the focal point of Jewish worship and culture. You will discover many fascinating details about the architecture, construction, and layout of the Temple Mount and the biblical events that took place in or near the temple. For example, you'll see:

- Where the City of David was located. Only about ten acres in size, this city played a key role during David's reign.

- Evidences of King Herod's genius. (Hand-hewn rocks his engineers positioned on the Temple Mount weigh more than 500 metric tons each.)

- The site where Peter and John healed the beggar (Acts 3:1 – 16).

- The location of the "Court of the Gentiles." You'll better understand why Jesus angrily drove the vendors and money-changers out of there.

The focus of this session is to gain a greater understanding of Jewish culture and spirituality in relationship to the temple and the events that transpired there. This is necessary because the material in this session and the following session on the city of Jerusalem provide background for the remaining sessions, which focus on events that took place in Jerusalem.

## Opening Thoughts (4 minutes)

### The Very Words of God

> Since the day I brought my people out of Egypt, I have not chosen a city in any tribe of Israel to have a temple built for my Name to be there, nor have I chosen anyone to be the leader over my people Israel. But now I have chosen Jerusalem for my Name to be there, and I have chosen David to rule my people Israel.
>
> *2 Chronicles 6:5 – 6*

**Think About It**

When we think about great cities we have visited or in which we have lived, there is often one place, event, or person that stands out as the symbol that identifies or represents what that city means to us.

In the minds of many people, the Temple Mount where God's temple once stood is the central symbol that identifies Jerusalem. When you think about all that has taken place in Jerusalem, which events that took place in the vicinity of the Temple Mount have had an impact on your Christian faith?

# DVD Teaching Notes (23 minutes)

### The topography of Jerusalem

### The Temple Mount

### Events within the temple

**A house of prayer for all nations**

## DVD Discussion (6 minutes)

Look at the diagram of the city of Jerusalem during Jesus' time, on page 107. Note the locations of the Temple Mount, the Royal Stoa, and David's City on the slope below.

1.  What did you learn about the city of Jerusalem or the Temple Mount that has changed your perception of what Jerusalem was like, or changed your understanding of what you have read in the Bible?

2.  Why was Herod's temple in Jerusalem so important to the Jews that it even had a court for lepers?

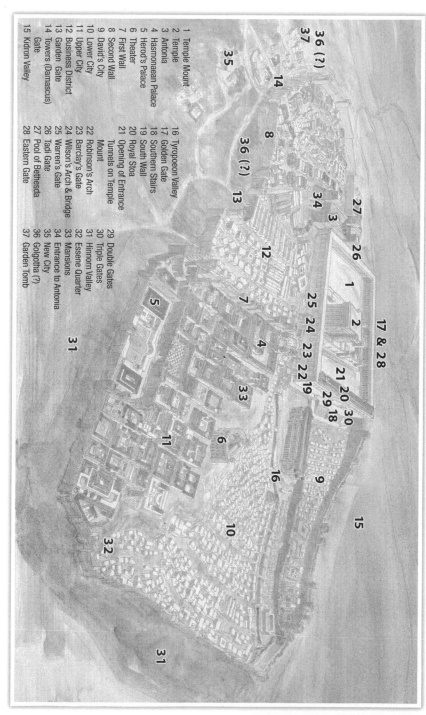

1 Temple Mount
2 Temple
3 Antonia
4 Hasmonaean Palace
5 Herod's Palace
6 Theater
7 First Wall
8 Second Wall
9 David's City
10 Lower City
11 Upper City
12 Business District
13 Garden Gate
14 Towers (Damascus) Gate
15 Kidron Valley

16 Tyropoeon Valley
17 Golden Gate
18 Southern Gate
19 Southern Stairs
20 South Wall
21 Royal Stoa
22 Opening of Entrance Tunnels on Temple Mount
23 Robinson's Arch
24 Barclay's Gate
25 Wilson's Arch & Bridge
26 Warren's Gate
27 Tadi Gate
28 Pool of Bethesda
28 Eastern Gate

29 Double Gates
30 Triple Gates
31 Hinnom Valley
32 Essene Quarter
33 Mansions
34 Entrance to Antonia
35 New City
36 Golgotha (?)
37 Garden Tomb

**JERUSALEM OF JESUS' TIME**

3. Imagine that you were one of the Sadducean priests who operated the temple. What might you have thought and how might you have responded when Jesus forced the buyers and sellers out of the temple's Gentile Court?

## Small Group Bible Discovery and Discussion (16 minutes)

### God Establishes His Presence among His People

It is an awesome thing to experience the presence of God. The Israelites were terrified of the thick smoke, consuming fire, trembling earth, and loud sounds when God came down to Mount Sinai to talk with Moses. They fell down in worship when the fire of the Lord consumed Elijah's sacrifice. So try to imagine the impact on God's people when he established his presence in the temple in Jerusalem!

1. What amazing promise did God make to Solomon regarding the temple? (See 1 Kings 6:11 – 13.)

   What condition had to be met for God to fulfill his promise?

   What do you think this says about the importance of living in the way God has decreed? About the price we pay when we pursue our own way?

2.  At the dedication of the temple, what did the priests place in the Holy of Holies? (See 1 Kings 8:6, 10 – 11; 2 Chronicles 5:7, 11 – 6:2; 7:1 – 3.)

    How did God make his presence known to all of Israel, and how did the people respond?

3.  During the Jewish feast of Pentecost after Jesus' death and resurrection, where did God's presence, as represented by tongues of fire, take up residence, and where does it dwell today? (See Acts 2:1 – 3; 1 Corinthians 3:16 – 17; 6:19 – 20.).

4.  As this brief study has shown, people often responded in dramatic ways when they saw evidence of God's presence with them. When was the last time you saw or heard of people responding in a dramatic way to the presence of God that was evident in the life of a Christian?

    Why do you think there is a difference, and do you think it indicates a problem? Why or why not?

## DATA FILE
### Solomon's Temple

Construction began about 950 BC on the Mount Moriah site chosen by David at God's leading—on a high point of the ridge known as David's City, just north of the original city.

- Construction took seven years.
- No hammers or chisels were used on-site; the stones were prepared at the quarry.
- It was built of limestone, parts of which were covered with gold and cedar.
- It was precisely and luxuriously furnished (1 Kings 7:13–51; 2 Chronicles 4).
- It held the ark of the covenant (1 Kings 8:1–21; 2 Chronicles 5).
- After its dedication to God (1 Kings 8:22–66; 2 Chronicles 6), the temple was filled by God's presence (2 Chronicles 5:13–14; 7:1–3).

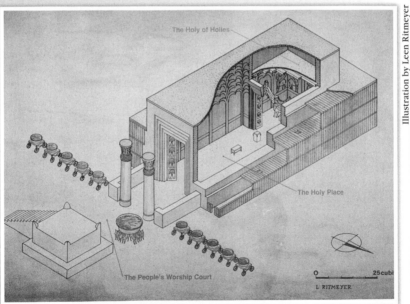

Illustration by Leen Ritmeyer

**THE FIRST TEMPLE AT JERUSALEM**

## Faith Lesson (5 minutes)

During ancient times, God often demonstrated his presence using visible signs such as fire and shining glory. Today, the Spirit of God whose presence filled the Holy of Holies in the temple now lives in every Christian! What an incredible opportunity we have to be used by God to reveal his presence if we will simply demonstrate our love for him through faithful obedience to his commands.

1. How do you believe God's promise to live among his people in the temple — if they would obey his commands — relates to Christians today?

   How committed are you to obeying God — in all areas of your life?

   In which areas do you need to make improvements?

2. Just as God's glorious presence filled the temple, his Spirit — revealed in "tongues of fire" at Pentecost — lives in every person who has accepted Jesus the Messiah as Lord and Savior. What does this say to you about the character of God and the kind of relationship he desires to have with you?

   Why is obedience such an important part of this relationship?

3. People often traveled great distances to be in the presence of God in Solomon's temple. What is your commitment to exhibiting his presence — the Holy Spirit who lives within every Christian — wherever you go and in whatever you do?

How well are you living up to this commitment?

In which areas do you need to make improvements?

## Closing (1 minute)

Read together 1 Corinthians 3:16: "Don't you know that you yourselves are God's temple and that God's Spirit lives in you?" Then pray, thanking God for choosing to live in the heart and life of every Christian. Tell him of your desire and commitment to obey him and to be a suitable temple that reveals the glory of his presence to the world around you.

### Memorize

*Don't you know that you yourselves are God's temple and that God's Spirit lives in you?*

*1 Corinthians 3:16*

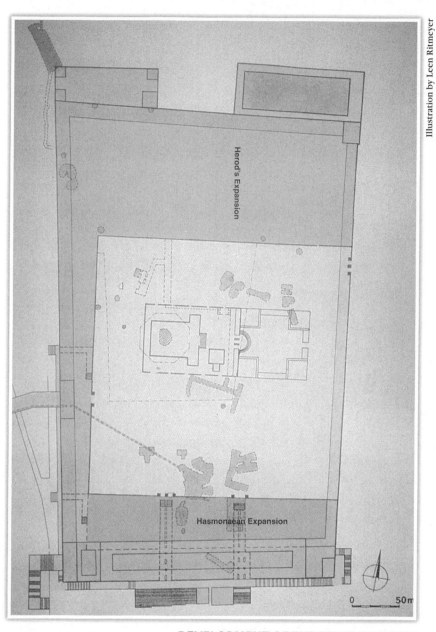

Illustration by Leen Ritmeyer

**DEVELOPMENT OF THE TEMPLE MOUNT**

# When Following Jesus Is the Most Important Thing in Life

*In-Depth Personal Study Sessions*

## Day One | Moriah: Mountain of Faith and Sacrifice

### The Very Words of God

> *Then Solomon began to build the temple of the* Lord *in Jerusalem on Mount Moriah, where the* Lord *had appeared to his father David. It was on the threshing floor of Araunah the Jebusite, the place provided by David. He began building on the second day of the second month in the fourth year of his reign.*
>
> *2 Chronicles 3:1 – 2*

### Bible Discovery

#### The Importance of Mount Moriah

Mount Moriah had been a part of Israel's heritage since the time of Abraham. God chose Mount Moriah to be the place where he would put his name, the place where his presence would live. The temple built on Mount Moriah was the focal point of Israel's faith. It was the place where people of all nations could come to worship the God of Israel. During the Roman occupation, temple worship was a unifying symbol for the Jewish people.

1.  For what reason did Abraham travel to the region of Moriah? What happened there? (See Genesis 22:1 – 14.)

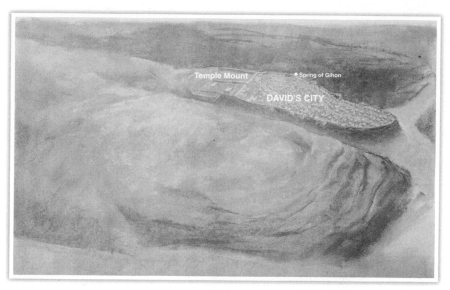

**JERUSALEM OF DAVID AND SOLOMON**

2.  Describe how David, after receiving a prophetic word from Gad — his prophet — selected the future site of the temple on Mount Moriah. How did God confirm his approval of the site? (See 1 Chronicles 21:18 – 26; 22:1.)

3.  What did David bring into his city on Mount Moriah? (See 2 Samuel 6:1 – 15.)

4.  Whom did God select to build the temple? What kind of a temple did he build? Where did he begin building it? (See 1 Chronicles 28:2 – 7; 2 Chronicles 2:5; 3:1.)

5. Which other event that changed lives and history took place near Jerusalem and Mount Moriah? (See Matthew 27:32 – 35.)

## Reflection

Events that happened on or near Mount Moriah reveal aspects of God's unfolding plan of salvation that culminated in Jesus' sacrifice on the cross for the sins of humanity.

What common threads link Abraham's experience on Mount Moriah, the Israelites' offering of sacrifices there, and Jesus' crucifixion?

How does your understanding of God's character and love for all people deepen as you begin to see these connections between Abraham, the nation of Israel, and Jesus? What impact does this have on you and your relationship with God?

How did Abraham, David, Solomon, and the people of Israel respond to what God had done, was doing, and would do in their lives in relationship to what took place on Mount Moriah?

Do you share in their joy, excitement, and desire to go "over the top" in honoring God because of who he is and what he has done? Why or why not?

The theme of sacrifice echoes throughout the Bible, as evident in the Scripture text in this study.

What has the need for coming to God and offering the sacrifices he requires shown you about the seriousness of sin?

How does it help you to better appreciate the sacrifice Jesus made for you on the cross?

What difference is his sacrifice making in how you live your life today?

# Day Two | Jesus in the Temple Courts

## The Very Words of God

*Every year his parents went to Jerusalem for the Feast of the Passover. When he was twelve years old, they went up to the Feast, according to the custom. After the Feast was over, while his parents were returning home, the boy Jesus stayed behind in Jerusalem, but they were unaware of it....*
*After three days they found him in the temple courts, sitting among the teachers, listening to them and asking them questions.*

*Luke 2:41 – 43, 46*

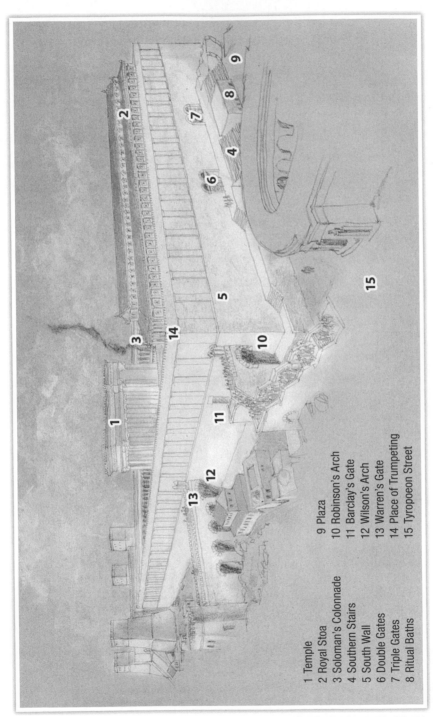

1 Temple
2 Royal Stoa
3 Soloman's Colonnade
4 Southern Stairs
5 South Wall
6 Double Gates
7 Triple Gates
8 Ritual Baths
9 Plaza
10 Robinson's Arch
11 Barclay's Gate
12 Wilson's Arch
13 Warren's Gate
14 Place of Trumpeting
15 Tyropoeon Street

**THE TEMPLE MOUNT: AD 70**

## Bible Discovery

### *Jesus and His Disciples Went to the Temple Courts Often*

By age twelve, Jesus knew the Scriptures thoroughly. So even at that young age, he used the opportunity to discuss them with Jewish religious leaders. Later, during his ministry, he and his disciples often went to the temple — the center of worship, prayer, and discussion of the Scriptures.

## DATA FILE
### Herod's Building of the Temple

Made of marble and gold, Herod's temple was taller than a fifteen-story building. The temple platform — the largest temple base in the ancient world — was more than 900 feet wide from east to west and more than 1,500 feet long from north to south. Built on the exact location of Solomon's temple and the temple Nehemiah reconstructed, it could accommodate hundreds of thousands of pilgrims at a time and was twice as large as the largest temple enclosure in Rome.

A thousand priests, trained as masons by Herod, worked on the temple, as did ten thousand highly skilled laborers using a thousand wagons. Some limestone blocks of the supporting platform weighed more than five hundred tons. Here is how the temple platform was laid out:

**The Eastern Wall** followed the original line dating from Solomon's days. The main feature in the wall, the Eastern Gate, was the original eastern entrance to the Temple Mount. At one point, the walls of the temple rose more than 225 feet above the bottom of the Kidron Valley.

**The South Wall** was more than 900 feet long and more than 150 feet high. Pilgrims entered the temple primarily through this entrance — the Double Gates — after climbing the Southern Stairs — a broad staircase more than two hundred feet wide.

*continued on next page . . .*

**The Western Wall** was a common gathering place during Jesus' time and featured various architectural wonders and gates. Some of these features, identified by their modern names, include:

- *Robinson's Arch*—One of the largest masonry arches (75 feet tall, more than 45 feet across) in the ancient world; supported a massive staircase that ran from the Tyropoeon Valley and the Lower City to the Royal Stoa (the place of buying and selling, the location of the temple treasury, and the Sanhedrin's meeting place); destroyed in AD 70 by the Romans.
- *Barclay's Gate*—Provided access to the Gentile Court from Tyropoeon Street.
- *Wilson's Arch*—Supported a bridge that extended from the Upper City, where the Sadducees and other influential Jews lived, across the Tyropoeon Valley to the Temple Mount; extended 75 feet above the valley floor and spanned 45 feet.
- *Warren's Gate*—Provided direct access to the temple courts from the West.
- *Massive Ashlars*—Hand-shaped stones brought from a quarry nearly a mile away. One 45-foot-long stone weighed nearly 600 tons. (See Mark 13:1–2; Luke 21:5.)

**The North Wall** is where the Antonia fortress was located. Built by Herod the Great, this fortress guarded the northern side of Jerusalem and, during Jesus' time, held Roman troops who watched the temple activities. Paul was probably brought to the Antonia after his arrest and defended himself on the stairs that apparently led to the fortress (Acts 21:27–40; 22:22–25).

The temple platform's extension to the west required enormous retaining walls on the south and west. Some of the rocks used in the wall weighed more than 500 tons each. The finished platform was divided into courts, which became increasingly more sacred the closer they were to the temple and the Holy of Holies.

1. Christians today know that Jesus taught throughout Galilee, but many do not realize how important the temple and its courts were in his life and ministry. How frequently (at least at one point in his ministry) did Jesus teach in the temple courts? (See Matthew 26:55.)

2. During Jesus' time, the temple was the center of religious life for the Jews. Crowds of people came to the temple and its courts to offer sacrifices and offerings, for cleansing, for teaching, and to pray. As you read the following examples, think about why Jesus spent time teaching in the temple, and notice how people responded to his message.

| Scripture Text | How Jesus' Message Was Received |
|---|---|
| Mark 11:27–28 | |
| Mark 12:35–37 | |
| Luke 2:41–47 | |
| John 7:14–16, 37–44 | |
| John 8:2–11 | |
| John 10:22–33 | |

3. Where did the early Christians meet and teach? Why? (See Acts 2:44 – 47; 5:17 – 32.)

4. Where did Peter heal a man who had been crippled since birth? (See Acts 3:1 – 16.)

Whose example did Peter follow? (See John 5:1 – 14.)

## PROFILES IN CONTRAST

| Herod the Great | Jesus |
|---|---|
| Built spectacular buildings: the temple in Jerusalem; Masada, a fortress in the Judea Wilderness; Jericho; and the seaport in Caesarea. | Built with people — living stones (Matthew 16:18; 1 Peter 2:4 – 8). |
| Built to honor himself. | Built for the honor of God. |
| His works lie in ruins today. | His projects will last forever. |

## Reflection

Today, most of us live fairly close to at least one church — a place to worship God. In Jesus' day, however, one location for worship was paramount: the temple in Jerusalem. People often traveled many miles to worship there (especially during the times commanded by God), and rabbis who taught in the temple courts found eager listeners.

Jesus highly valued opportunities to teach and worship in the temple. Where do you go to join with other Christians in worshiping God and learning more about him?

How greatly do you value these opportunities?

To what extent does the teaching in your faith community focus on understanding the meaning of Scripture and knowing how to obey it in daily life?

Why is it important for Christians to know and obey the Scriptures?

The early Christians followed Jesus' example and continued meeting in the temple for worship and teaching. How important is it for you to discover more about the heart of God and his desire to bring salvation to all people through the structures, worship practices, and history of God's temple in Jerusalem?

What will you do to continue learning the ways in which the Christian faith is rooted in ancient Jewish culture?

## Memorize

*Each day Jesus was teaching at the temple, and each evening he went out to spend the night on the hill called the Mount of Olives, and all the people came early in the morning to hear him at the temple.*

*Luke 21:37 – 38*

# Day Three | The Soreq — and Other Dividing Walls within the Temple

## The Very Words of God

*I am not ashamed of the gospel, because it is the power of God for the salvation of everyone who believes: first for the Jew, then for the Gentile.*

*Romans 1:16*

## Bible Discovery

### *The Power of Salvation Breaks Down the Separation between Jew and Gentile*

The *Soreq*, a five-foot-tall stone wall that surrounded the inner courts of the consecrated temple area, was designed to keep Gentiles and other "unacceptable" people out of the inner courts. Gentiles could not pass the Soreq on pain of death. When the salvation message initially was proclaimed to everyone — both Jew and Gentile — some of the early Jewish believers, even some of Jesus' disciples, resisted the inclusion of Gentiles.

1. Of what crime related to the Soreq was Paul accused, and how did he respond to the accusation? (See Acts 21:27 – 22:21.)

## THE TEMPLE COURTS

In addition to the Soreq, there were many other walls and divisions within the temple and its courts. (See the diagram on page 126.) Each had its purpose and specific limitations as to who could enter it and under which circumstances. Each court was progressively exclusive as it approached the Holy of Holies. The separations were indicated by each of the following:

| The Court | Who Was Allowed to Enter |
|---|---|
| The Gentile Court | Largest area of the temple platform where Gentiles were allowed to pray and listen to the teaching of the rabbis; where Jesus threw out the money changers and sellers. |
| The Court of the Women | Area inside the Soreq but outside the temple building, which was as close as women were allowed to the temple. |
| Chamber of Nazirites | Adjacent to the Court of the Women, for Nazirites who had been set apart for service to God. |
| Chamber of Lepers | Adjacent to the Court of the Women, where lepers could worship and be declared "clean"; had to be separate because lepers were unclean. |
| Court of the Israelites | Closer to the temple building than the Court of the Women; for men over age twelve only. |
| Court of the Priests | Closest to the temple building; where sacrifices were offered; priests were separated by their calling to represent the people to God. |
| Sanctuary of the Temple | Inside the temple building, which could be entered only by priests and Levites; separated the people from the presence of God. |
| The Holy of Holies | The holiest part of the temple, to be entered only by the high priest on Yom Kippur; location of the ark of the covenant; the veil separated the presence of God from the priests. |

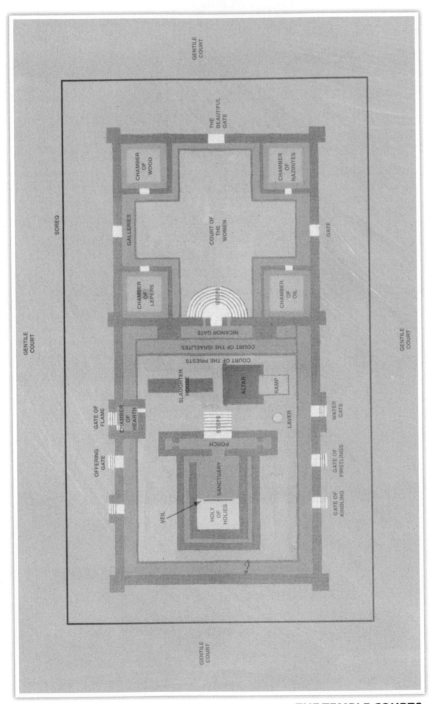

**THE TEMPLE COURTS**

2.  Later, in Ephesians 2:14 – 16, what did Paul say had been destroyed?

    When he used that phrase, what other kinds of "walls" might he have been describing?

3.  Peter was passionate about following Jesus. He was one of the disciples who had to be convinced that salvation eliminated the separation between Jew and Gentile (Acts 10:25 – 11:21).

    a.  What message did God give to Peter concerning the Gentiles and the walls that had existed between the Jews and Gentiles? (See Acts 10:25 – 43.)

    b.  What did God do to confirm to Peter (and everyone else who saw it) that "everyone who believes in him receives forgiveness of sins through his name"? (See Acts 10:44 – 48.)

    c.  How did Peter explain to the believers in Jerusalem what God had shown him about the Gentile believers, and how did they respond? (See Acts 11:4 – 18.)

d.  In what way did God again show that the gospel message was for all people — Jews and Gentiles? (See Acts 11:19 – 21.)

4.  Despite God's outpouring of blessing among Gentiles, some Jews began to insist that the Gentiles were still required to obey Moses' law. How did the apostles reply? (See Acts 15:5 – 19; Amos 9:11 – 12. See also Isaiah 45:21; 54:1 – 5.)

How does their discussion reflect their deep knowledge of the Scriptures and understanding of God's desire to reconcile all people unto himself?

## Reflection

It took a while for Jews and Gentiles to realize that the gospel message of salvation through Jesus the Messiah was for all of them. The symbolic wall between them was gone. Sadly, though, similar walls sometimes exist in our day — walls of pride, economic status, race, social status, bitterness, and so on.

If Paul were alive today, which walls do you think he would point out that divide us from other people?

What has been your role in maintaining these divisions?

What would God have you do to break down walls that divide you from other people?

What specific ideas do you have for bringing together people who love Jesus with people who may be curious about him or have serious spiritual interests, but do not know him?

What steps will you take to broaden your horizons and invite people who are presently outside the community of believers to come in, discover, and worship God?

## Memorize

*There is neither Jew nor Greek, slave nor free, male nor female, for you are all one in Christ Jesus. If you belong to Christ, then you are Abraham's seed, and heirs according to the promise.*

**Galatians 3:28 – 29**

## Day Four | The Temple — A House of Prayer for All Nations

## The Very Words of God

*For my house will be called a house of prayer for all nations.*

**Isaiah 56:7**

### Bible Discovery

## God's Temple Was for Gentiles, Too

The temple in Jerusalem symbolized both the presence of God and the way to God. The Jews, as the people of the covenant, were allowed into the inner courts of the temple to offer sacrifices and worship. But God also provided a way for people who were not Jews to commit themselves to him. He delighted in sharing his presence with his chosen people, and he welcomed Gentiles who loved and served him to come into the Gentile Court surrounding the temple to pray and worship.

1. God's plan of salvation has always been for the whole world. What did God want Gentiles who loved and served him to experience in his temple? (See Isaiah 56:3 – 7.)

2. A beautiful colonnade named the Royal Stoa spanned the southern end of the temple platform. During the time of Jesus, this was the area where transactions for temple sacrifices took place. However, the booths for buying and selling sacrifices, the inspection of animals, and the changing of foreign currencies — all of which were operated by Sadducean priests — overflowed into the Gentile Court. These activities apparently interfered with the Gentiles' worship of the one true God.

   a. What did Jesus do in the Royal Stoa after his triumphant entry into Jerusalem? (See Matthew 21:12 – 13; Luke 19:45 – 46; John 2:13 – 16.)

    b.   What apparently motivated Jesus to take this drastic action, and why would this have been important to him? (See Isaiah 56:7.)

    c.   What did Jesus' disciples recognize about him when he did this, and what impact do you think it had on them? (See John 2:17.)

## Reflection

God wanted his temple — the symbol of his presence on earth — to be available to everyone. He delights in every person who comes to him in prayer and worship. So Jesus took strong action against religious leaders who hindered hurting, sinful, "unclean" people who desired to experience the presence of God.

> What might Christians (and that includes each of us individually) be doing that would kindle Jesus' anger in a similar way?

> What are you doing in your everyday life (remember, you are the temple of God today) to give people the opportunity to know Jesus and experience God's presence?

> What are some new ways in which you can become more sensitive to people's spiritual needs and make the presence of God more accessible to people? For example, could you

get involved in local outreach to needy people? Or become active in a local political concern? Or start a neighborhood outreach?

In which ways might you be holding back the love God wants you to express to sinful, hurting, broken people? Are you just too busy? Is it too uncomfortable for you? Have you hardened your heart to "outsiders" whom God loves?

Some Jewish believers in the early church didn't want the gospel preached to the Gentiles. Can you think of certain individuals or groups of people with whom Christians today have deliberately not shared the gospel?

What Jesus would think about that is obvious. What do you think about it, and what will you do about it?

## Memorize

*It is too small a thing for you to be my servant to restore the tribes of Jacob and bring back those of Israel I have kept. I will also make you a light for the Gentiles, that you may bring my salvation to the ends of the earth.*

**Isaiah 49:6**

## BACKGROUND NOTES
### The Pharisees

- Derived their name from the word *perushim*, which meant "separated" or "separatists."

- Tried to be devoted to God without resorting to violence against the Romans.

- Devoted themselves to obeying every detail of Jewish law and separating themselves from all influences or people who might interfere with that devotion.

- Believed that Moses had given a two-part law — the written law of the Torah and additional oral commandments that had been passed through generations to help the faithful understand and apply the written law.

- The Pharisees interpreted and greatly expanded the oral law, which became a detailed guide to living obediently every day. Their intent was to help people understand the Torah, in much the same way that Christians use a creed or catechism to help summarize and interpret the Bible.

- Believed in angels, the physical resurrection of the dead, a coming day of judgment, the coming of Messiah, and a loving God who desired a life of obedience.

- Recognized a combination of free choice and divine control in human life.

- Had some people within their ranks who were hypocritical or became so focused on obedience that they did not notice or care about the needs of other people. Jesus never criticized anyone for being a Pharisee and instructed his followers to obey what the Pharisees taught (Matthew 23:2–3). Jesus only criticized "hypocritical" ones (Matthew 23) and those who spoiled the whole group (Matthew 16:6, 11.) In fact, many Pharisees supported Jesus, tried to protect him (Luke 13:31), and became Jesus' followers (Acts 15:5).

- Obtained their authority by knowledge and piety.

*continued on next page . . .*

## The Sadducees

- After Israel returned from the Babylonian captivity, it was the tradition that the high priest must be from the tribe of Levi, the family of Aaron, and the family of Zadok—Solomon's high priest (1 Kings 2:35; Ezekiel 40:46). Descendants of this family, *Zedukim* (or "Sadducee" in English) were the temple authorities throughout the time before Jesus was born. Descendants of Zadok and their supporters were also called "Sadducees."

- Although there may have been fewer than a thousand of them, they wielded great power.

- Were wealthy, politically active, and had a majority in the Sanhedrin—the religious council used by the Romans and Herods as the instrument to govern the Jewish people.

- Controlled the economy of the temple, often using their position for personal gain (Mark 11:15–18). In AD 15, they allowed the business of buying and selling to extend beyond the Royal Stoa and into the Gentile Court, a move that the Pharisees opposed.

- Many were Hellenistic but faithful to temple rituals.

- Believed the written Torah alone was authoritative, rejected oral law, hated the Pharisees, denied bodily resurrection and most Pharisaic doctrines of angels and spirits, and believed that the synagogue and study of the Torah as a form of worship undermined temple ritual.

- Obtained their authority by position and birth.

- Frequently dealt brutally with anyone who undermined the temple, its economy (their income), and its ritual.

- Had the most to lose because of Jesus. Any popular movement jeopardized their place as the majority on the Sanhedrin and the support of the Romans who ruled through it (John 11:49–53).

- Ceased to exist as a group after the temple in Jerusalem was destroyed.

## **Day Five** | The Temple, God's House of Prayer

### The Very Words of God

> *For the eyes of the Lord are on the righteous and his ears are attentive to their prayer.*
>
> 1 Peter 3:12

### Bible Discovery

### *God Listens When His People Pray*

God promised to hear the prayers of his people in his temple, the dwelling place of his presence. So they went to the temple to offer praise and to seek forgiveness. They went there to ask for healing, deliverance, peace, and prosperity. Today, there is no temple of stone where God's people go to pray, but God still desires to commune with his people; he still listens when his people pray.

1. One reason the temple was built was to provide a dwelling place for God's presence. The temple was the place where God could live among his people and commune with them. Solomon's prayer of dedication for the temple he built for God provides a beautiful picture of what the ongoing conversation between God and his people could be like. Read Solomon's prayer in 2 Chronicles 6:16 – 42, then answer the following:

   a. What was Solomon's response to the prospect of God's presence actually dwelling with God's people?

   b. What kind of two-way communication did he envision taking place between God and his people?

    c.   What did he ask God to do for the foreigners who would pray at the temple, and why?

2.  After hearing Solomon's prayer of dedication, what did God promise? (See 2 Chronicles 7:11 – 22.)

How attentive had God been to Solomon's prayer?

3.  The Jewish people consistently came into the temple to be in the presence of God, to communicate their prayers of praise and petition, and to hear his response. As you read the following passages of Scripture, note the connection between the place God dwells and prayer.

| Scripture Text | Prayer in the Presence of God |
|---|---|
| Ps. 27:1–6 | |
| Ps. 99:1–9 | |
| Ps. 122:1–4 | |
| Isa. 37:14–22 | |

4.  The pages of Scripture are filled with accounts of how God listens to and responds to the prayers of his people. Prayer is the essential dialogue between God and his people, but

many Christians today underestimate its importance. Perhaps the following passages will help us to adjust our perceptions of the value of prayer.

a.   What do the words of Moses in Deuteronomy 4:7 reveal about the privilege of prayer?

b.   What does the prophet Jeremiah reveal about the hope of prayer? (See Jeremiah 29:11 – 13.)

c.   What does Matthew 6:5 – 13 reveal about the purpose and practice of prayer?

d.   What does Romans 8:26 – 27 reveal about our need for prayer?

## Reflection

It is an amazing truth to consider, but the infinite and sovereign Ruler of the universe cherishes the prayers of his people! Before the temple was built, while it was in use, and after it was destroyed, God's people have always related to him through prayer.

Ancient Jews and Gentiles sometimes traveled for many days just to pray and worship in the temple in Jerusalem. How might your ongoing conversation with God be more meaningful and effective if you, in effect, "went up to God's temple" by setting aside a specific time and place in which to pray?

How much would you like to have the kind of prayer conversation that Solomon and God had when the temple was dedicated?

What do you think is required for that to happen?

What effort and sacrifice would such a conversation be worth to you?

Many Christians today don't see the essential connection between prayer and obedience to God's commands. But think about it. Can you imagine an intimate, meaningful conversation with the God of the universe, the author of salvation, if you don't see eye-to-eye on how he wants his people to live? Why or why not?

What disobedience to God may be hindering your prayer relationship with him? What will you, with the help of his Spirit, do about it?

# A CHRONOLOGY OF TEMPLE EVENTS

| | |
|---|---|
| Approximately 2000 BC | Abraham was sent to the Moriah area to sacrifice Isaac. Jerusalem was later built on the mountain named Moriah. |
| Approximately 1000 BC | David captured the Canaanite city of Jebus (2 Samuel 5:6–7) and named it the City of David, which he made his capital (1 Chronicles 11:7). He selected the temple site at the threshing floor of Araunah on Mount Moriah, where he built an altar. |
| Approximately 950 BC | Solomon built the temple on the Mount Moriah site chosen by David at God's leading. After the ark of the covenant, the resting place of God's glorious presence, was moved into the temple (God's earthly home), the people prayed for God's presence (2 Chronicles 6) and God sent fire to consume their sacrifices (2 Chronicles 7:1–3). |
| 586 BC | The Babylonians destroyed the temple and took many Israelites captive. |
| Approximately 500 BC | Cyrus, king of Persia, decreed that the Israelites could return to Jerusalem. Under Ezra and Nehemiah's leadership, the temple was rebuilt (Ezra 1:1–4; 3:7–13; 6:15). Since there was no ark of the covenant, the Holy of Holies was left empty. The Jews rejoiced when the Torah was read (Nehemiah 8:17). |
| 322 BC | Jerusalem, rebuilt during Ezra's time, became part of Alexander the Great's empire. The city suffered more than a century of conflict at the hands of Alexander's Hellenistic successors. Antiochus, the king of the Syrians, outlawed the Sabbath, circumcision, the study of Torah, and even defiled the great altar by sacrificing pigs on it. |
| 165 BC | The Maccabean revolt against the Greek army brought Jerusalem back under Jewish control. The menorah—the symbol of eternal light in the Holy of Holies—was relit. Descendants of the Maccabees expanded the Temple Mount. The city now covered 175 acres and had more than 30,000 inhabitants. |
| 63 BC | The Romans took control of Judea. |
| 37–4 BC | Herod, the king of Israel appointed by Rome, lavishly expanded the Temple Mount, embellished the temple, fortified the city, and built many spectacular buildings. A wonder of the ancient world, the city was now ready for the ministry of Jesus, the Messiah. But Herod also conducted a reign of terror designed to keep the Jewish people in line. To keep his position, Herod needed the might of Rome, the support of the Sadducees (the temple authorities), and the favor of Hellenistic Jews. Afraid of losing his throne to the Messiah, Herod killed the male babies in Bethlehem (Matthew 2:16). |

*continued on next page . . .*

| | |
|---|---|
| Approximately AD 30 | The Sadducees had Jesus crucified, at which time the veil separating the inner chamber of the temple (the Holy of Holies) split from top to bottom, symbolizing the access all people now had to God's presence through Jesus. On the Christian fulfillment of Pentecost, God took up residence in a new temple — his community of believers (1 Corinthians 3:16–17). The disciples continued to meet and teach in the temple courts. |
| AD 44 | Herod Agrippa I, grandson of Herod the Great, died. Rebel Jews began killing Romans and Jews who cooperated with them, and Roman governors became increasingly cruel. The temple priesthood, more dependent than ever on the Romans for security and support, became more corrupt. |
| AD 66 | A Gentile offered a "pagan" sacrifice next to the synagogue's entrance in Caesarea. The Jerusalem authorities decided to end all foreign sacrifices. The Rome-appointed governor, Florus, authorized Roman troops to raid the temple treasury. When the Jews protested, Florus's troops killed many innocent civilians. In turn, Jewish mobs drove out the Roman troops, stormed the Antonia (the Roman fort), and occupied the fortress of Masada. When the Romans in Caesarea learned what had happened, they killed 20,000 Jews within a day's time. |
| AD 68 | Ultra-nationalistic Jews (the Zealots) appointed their own temple priest and slaughtered the Sadducean priests who resisted. |
| AD 70 | Under Titus, at least 80,000 Roman troops destroyed Jerusalem, slaughtering hundreds of thousands of Jews. The streets ran with Jewish blood. On August 9, the temple was burned and destroyed. All the citizens of Jerusalem (more than one million) were executed, sold into slavery, or captured for games in the arena. |
| AD 131 | A second Jewish revolt started, driving Christianity to the ends of the earth, where it soon became a largely Gentile faith. Only today are the Jewish roots of Christianity being fully appreciated. |
| AD 135 | Rome squashed the second revolt, outlawed the Jewish religion, and Judea became Palestine. Rabbinic Judaism became the Orthodox faith of Jewish people today. The Jews became a people without a country. |

# CITY OF THE GREAT KING — JERUSALEM

To the Jewish people who lived during the time of Jesus, there was no city like Jerusalem. The soul-stirring events that took place within its walls and on the Temple Mount had deep cultural and religious significance. Influential leaders such as David, Hezekiah, Nehemiah, Solomon, and others had made significant marks on their culture — and even on the world — while living in Jerusalem, and their great deeds had been recorded for generations to remember. Even before Jerusalem became a city, God had spoken to Abraham and Isaac there. God later allowed David to prepare for the temple and commissioned Solomon to build it in that holy city. But few Jews living during Jesus' time could have imagined what God was about to accomplish in their bustling city.

In Bethlehem, about six miles from Jerusalem, a child named Jesus was born. He grew up in Nazareth, about sixty miles (as the crow flies) from Jerusalem, and as soon as he was old enough began worshiping his heavenly Father in the temple. Jesus, the King of the universe, joined thousands of pilgrims who came every year to celebrate Passover, Pentecost, Hanukkah, and the Feast of Tabernacles in Jerusalem. In this magnificent city the chosen Lamb of God participated in temple ceremonies and taught Scripture.

Jesus centered his ministry in Capernaum, about seventy-five miles from Jerusalem, but the time came when he turned his focus toward Jerusalem and what he would accomplish there.

Just outside the city walls, God would demonstrate the greatest act of love and redemption the world would ever know. There, by a hill outside the city walls, Jesus ascended his throne by way of a cross — and the world forever changed for both Jews and Gentiles. Thus Jerusalem, the city of great kings, will always be remembered as the city of the eternal King of kings — our Messiah, Jesus.

Jerusalem's rich heritage provides an opportunity to visualize more fully God's great redemptive work. The more we learn about Jerusalem, the more we understand about God's power and love. We see how he has worked throughout history to bring his plans to fruition. With this purpose in mind, this video provides insights into:

- Herod's marvelous construction of what has come to be called Robinson's Arch.

- What Herod the Great's palace looked like (the palace where the wise men who sought Jesus probably met with Herod the Great, and where Herod Antipas probably interrogated Jesus after his arrest).

- The lifestyle of influential religious leaders. The ruins of an opulent mansion reveal what Jesus may have seen when the Jewish leaders interrogated him in Caiaphas's home.

- The city walls within which Jesus conducted a portion of his ministry and the areas of the city that Jesus likely passed through on market day as he carried his cross.

- The horror of the Romans' destruction of Jerusalem in AD 70, which caused Jesus to weep when he foresaw it.

- The huge fortress — the Antonia — that Herod the Great built to protect the city and house the Roman garrison.

## Opening Thoughts (4 minutes)

*The Very Words of God*

> *It is beautiful in its loftiness, the joy of the whole earth. Like the utmost heights of Zaphon is Mount Zion, the city of the Great King.*
>
> **Psalm 48:2**

### Think About It

Think for a moment about the times you have explored great historical sites — perhaps the site of the Battle of Gettysburg, the great castles of Europe, the ruins of ancient communities in the Middle East, China's Great Wall — or viewed a reenactment of a great event. When we see these things, we often imagine what life would have been like as the significant events that took place there unfolded.

What do you imagine life would have been like for you in Jerusalem during Jesus' time? What sights, sounds, fears, hopes, joys, and struggles might you have experienced if you had lived in Jerusalem when Jesus worshiped, taught, healed, died, and rose again?

## DVD Teaching Notes (20 minutes)

### Features of the city districts

### Herod's palace

**The Jewish mansion**

**The Antonia**

**Jesus: our scapegoat**

## DVD Discussion (7 minutes)

Refer to the map of Jerusalem's Districts on page 145. Note the various districts of the city, and the locations of the Mount of Olives, the Temple Mount, the Eastern Gate, Herod's Palace, the Jewish mansions, the Antonia, and the Garden Gate.

1.  In our previous session, we explored the ancient temple and learned a bit about the Jews' religious practices, the temple history, and Jesus' ministry in the temple. Today, we looked at other historical sites and events in Jerusalem. Which sites or events in Jerusalem's three-thousand-plus years of history inspire you today?

A   David's City
B   New City
C   Upper City
D   Business District
E   Temple Mount
F   Lower City
G   Herod's Palace

1   Eastern Gate
2   Southern Gate
3   Royal Stoa
4   Robinson's Arch
5   Wilson's Arch
6   Tyropoeon Street
7   Warren's Gate
8   Antonia
9   Tadi Gate
10   Pool of Bethesda
11   Second Wall
12   First Wall
13   Garden Gate
14   Towers
15   Golgotha (?)
16   Garden Tomb
17   Spring of Gihon
18   Hinnom Valley
19   Theatre
20   Citadel and Herod's palace
21   Essence Quarter
22   Mansions
23   Mount of Olives
24   Kidron Valley
25   Huldah Gates

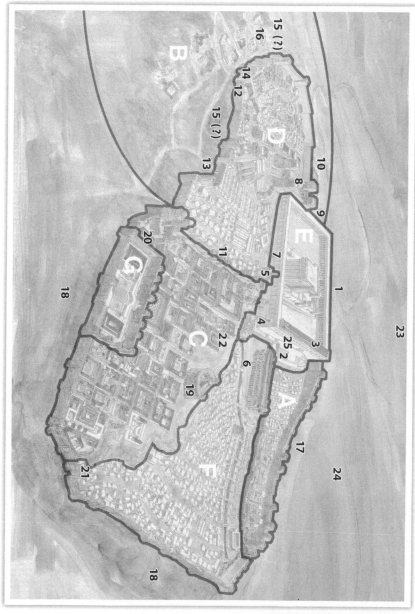

**JERUSALEM'S DISTRICTS**

2. Explain what you think it would have been like to have been an ordinary Jewish person who lived in a city ruled by the temple authorities, Herod, and the Romans.

In what ways has your understanding of what life was like during Jesus' day changed as a result of what you have seen?

Did you expect to see in Jerusalem a palace like Herod's, a fort like the Antonia, or fine mansions in which a priestly family may have lived? What were your expectations?

3. What are some of the images of Jerusalem you think Jesus might have had in mind when he wept over the city? What feelings do those images stir up in you?

## DATA FILE
### The Geographic Features and Events of Jerusalem
#### *Hinnom Valley*

The Hinnom Valley formed the western boundary of the Western Hill and the Upper City of Jesus' time; it began along the Western Hill and ended where the Tyropoeon and Kidron Valleys met. Here the kings and people of Judah sacrificed their children to Baal (2 Kings 23:10; 2 Chronicles 28:3–4; 33:1, 6; Jeremiah 7:31; 19:5–6; 32:35) and burned Jerusalem's garbage. Hinnom became a synonym for hell itself (Matthew 5:22, 29; 10:28; 18:9; 23:33; Mark 9:43–48; James 3:6).

#### *Kidron Valley*

The Kidron Valley is a deep wadi about three miles long, east of the city between David's City and the Mount of Olives. David crossed here when fleeing Absalom (2 Samuel 15:13–24); various kings destroyed idols and pagan objects here (1 Kings 15:11–12; 2 Kings 23:4–7, 12–14; 2 Chronicles 15:16); Jesus crossed here on his way to Gethsemane just before his

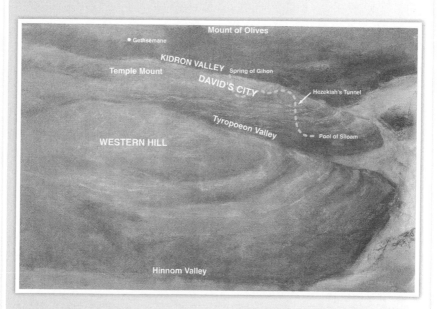

**TOPOGRAPHY OF JERUSALEM**

*continued on next page . . .*

arrest (John 18:1); Joel prophesied concerning the judgment of nations in the Valley of Jehoshaphat—believed to be part or all of this valley (Joel 3:2, 12); and Solomon refused to allow Shimei to cross here (1 Kings 2:36–38). Hezekiah's tunnel brought fresh water from the Spring of Gihon, which was in the valley, to the Pool of Siloam.

### Mount of Olives

The Mount of Olives is the highest peak in the area. David went here to escape Absalom's revolt (2 Samuel 15:13–37); Jesus entered Jerusalem from here (Matthew 21:1–11; Luke 19:1, 28–44), gave his final teaching here (Matthew 24:3–46), and ascended to heaven from here (Luke 24:50–52; Acts 1:6–12). This may be the location for Jesus' return (Zechariah 14:4; Acts 1:11).

### Tyropoeon Valley

The Tyropoeon Valley is between David's City and the Western Hill where the Upper City was located. Hezekiah expanded Jerusalem into this valley; the western wall of Herod's Gentile Court was located here, as was the Pool of Siloam where Jesus sent a blind man to wash (John 9:1–12); Nehemiah's workers repaired the wall near the Pool of Siloam (Nehemiah 3:15).

### Western Hill

Now called Mount Zion, the Western Hill was called the "Upper City" during Jesus' time. This was the site of Herod's palace; probably where the wise men talked with Herod the Great (Matthew 2:1–7), where Herod Antipas met Jesus (Luke 23:6–7), and where the Upper Room was located (Luke 22:7–13; Acts 1:12–13).

## Small Group Bible Discovery and Discussion (18 minutes)

*Jesus Heals at the Pool of Bethesda*

During his frequent visits to Jerusalem, there is little doubt that Jesus often passed by the pool of Bethesda. The pool was believed to have healing powers, so many disabled people who had little hope of being made whole other than through a miracle would gather there. Let's take a look at one life-changing miracle that Jesus performed at this site.

1.　On the map of Jerusalem's Districts (page 145), locate the Sheep Gate, also called Tadi Gate, on Jerusalem's northern wall. Next locate the Pool of Bethesda, which is just north of the Sheep Gate.

　　Given the reputation of the pool of Bethesda, its proximity to the temple, and its size (surrounded by five covered colonnades), how quickly do you think news of a healing there would spread through Jerusalem?

2.　Read the story of how Jesus healed the paralyzed man (John 5:1 – 14).

　　a.　Who would come to the pool of Bethesda and why? (See John 5:1 – 7.)

　　b.　Which aspect of Jesus' character was touched by what he saw at the pool, and how did he respond? (See John 5:6 – 9.)

　　c.　How much did the paralyzed man know about Jesus, and how quickly did he do what Jesus said? (See John 5:11 – 13.)

    d.  After being healed, where did the man go, and why do you think he went there? (See John 5:8 – 9, 14.)

3.  Although this story looks self-explanatory on the surface, it raises some questions that bear discussion.

    a.  Jesus was on his way to the temple to worship on the Sabbath during one of the Jewish feasts when he "stopped by" the pool of Bethesda. Why do you think Jesus went to the pool at that time?

    b.  While Jesus was at the pool, what did he learn about the paralyzed man? How do you think he learned this? How long do you think Jesus was there, and what might he have been doing?

    c.  Why do you think the paralyzed man, who didn't even know who Jesus was, responded so quickly to Jesus' healing command? Do you think this was an expression of his faith in God? Why or why not?

## Faith Lesson (5 minutes)

As we take time to explore what Jesus did, where he did it, and how he interacted with the people involved, the facts of Scripture come alive to us. We begin to connect historical events with places and people that are meaningful to us. Even more important, we better understand the heart of Jesus and the people to whom he ministered.

1. After the man was healed, he saw Jesus in the temple and discovered who Jesus was. At that time, Jesus admonished him to stop sinning.

   a. Have you experienced an unusual blessing from God that you at first did not recognize as coming from him? If so, how did you respond when you realized what God had done for you?

   b. When God provides for us in miraculous ways, how often is he trying to convey a message to us? What kinds of messages has he conveyed to you in this manner?

   c. After he was healed, the man went to the temple where the Jews prayed, worshiped, and offered sacrifices to God. What changes take place in your relationship with God when you comprehend the greatness of what he has done for you and seek to worship and obey him with your whole heart?

2. How does what you have seen and discussed today impact your view of Jesus and what he accomplished in the lives and hearts of people in Jerusalem?

# Closing (1 minute)

Read together Psalm 143:1 – 2, 8: "O LORD, hear my prayer, listen to my cry for mercy; in your faithfulness and righteousness come to my relief. Do not bring your servant into judgment, for no one living is righteous before you.... Let the morning bring me word of your unfailing love, for I have put my trust in you. Show me the way I should go, for to you I lift up my soul." Then pray, thanking God for his compassion and mercy in healing not only the body, but also the soul. Thank him for revealing who he is through the people, places, and events of the Bible. Ask him for a heart of understanding and faithfulness as you seek to live for him in the days ahead.

## Memorize

> O LORD, hear my prayer, listen to my cry for mercy; in your faithfulness and righteousness come to my relief. Do not bring your servant into judgment, for no one living is righteous before you.... Let the morning bring me word of your unfailing love, for I have put my trust in you. Show me the way I should go, for to you I lift up my soul.
>
> **Psalm 143:1 – 2, 8**

# When Following Jesus Is the Most Important Thing in Life

*In-Depth Personal Study Sessions*

## Day One | God Preserves Jerusalem, His Holy City

### The Very Words of God

> *When you go to war against your enemies and see horses and chariots and an army greater than yours, do not be afraid of them, because the LORD your God, who brought you up out of Egypt, will be with you.... For the LORD your God is the one who goes with you to fight for you against your enemies to give you victory.*
>
> *Deuteronomy 20:1, 4*

### Bible Discovery

### God Is Faithful to Accomplish His Purposes

During King Hezekiah's reign over Judah, he prepared for an attack on Jerusalem by Assyria, a powerful, brutal, pagan nation. Led by Sennacherib, the Assyrian army was strong and proud. They had defeated nation after nation and had utterly destroyed the northern kingdom of Israel in 722 BC. Hezekiah, however, placed his trust in God to defend his holy city, his people, and his honor.

1. What kind of a king was Hezekiah? (See 2 Chronicles 29:1 – 11, 35 – 36; 31:1, 20 – 21.)

2. What did Assyria do during the fourteenth year of King Hezekiah's reign? (See 2 Kings 18:13; Isaiah 36:1.)

## DATA FILE
## The Development of Jerusalem

| | |
|---|---|
| 2000 BC (circa) | God sends Abraham to the area of Mount Moriah to sacrifice Isaac. (The temple and part of Jerusalem is built on the mountain ridge named Moriah.) |
| 1000 BC (circa) | David captures Jerusalem (then the Canaanite city of Jebus), names it the City of David, and makes it his capital (2 Samuel 5:6–7; 1 Chronicles 11:4–7). The city is about ten acres in size and is home to about 1,500 people. |
| 950 BC (circa) | Solomon spends seven years building the temple, then spends thirteen years building his lavish palace (1 Kings 6:37–7:12), apparently between the temple and David's City. The city has about 4,500 people and covers approximately thirty acres. |
| 700 BC (circa) | Hezekiah expands Jerusalem—west across the Tyropoeon Valley onto the Western Hill—and fortifies the city against the Babylonian threat by building walls and tearing down houses in order to expand the walls (2 Chronicles 32:1–5; Isaiah 22:10). The city at that time covered about 100 acres and housed about 24,000 people. |
| 500 BC (circa) | The Babylonians capture Jerusalem, destroy the temple, and take many Israelites captive. |
| 430 BC (circa) | Cyrus, king of Persia, allows the Israelites to return to Jerusalem. They rebuild the temple and restore and dedicate the city walls (Nehemiah 2:1–8; 3; 12:27–47). |
| 322 BC | Jerusalem becomes part of Alexander the Great's empire. The city suffers more than a century of conflict at the hands of Alexander's successors. |
| 165 BC | The Maccabean revolt brings Jerusalem back under Jewish control. Descendants of the Maccabees enclose the Western Hill, build the fortress Baris (later the Antonia), and expand the Gentile Court. The city now covers 175 acres and has more than 30,000 inhabitants. |
| 63 BC | The Romans under Pompey capture Jerusalem from the Hasmonaeans (Maccabean descendants) and eventually place the city and country under Herod's control. |
| 37–4 BC | Herod the Great expands the Gentile Court, lavishly embellishes the temple, fortifies the city, and builds many structures. A wonder of the ancient world, the city has expanded to nearly 250 acres and has a population of about 45,000. |
| 70 AD | Under Titus, at least 80,000 Roman troops destroy Jerusalem, slaughtering hundreds of thousands of Jews. The streets run with Jewish blood. On August 9, the temple is burned and destroyed. All the citizens of Jerusalem (more than one million) are executed, sold into slavery, or captured for games in the arena. |

3. What had Hezekiah done to prepare for the Assyrian attack against Jerusalem? (See 2 Kings 20:20; 2 Chronicles 32:1 – 8.)

4. How did Hezekiah respond upon receiving the Assyrians' ultimatum? (See Isaiah 37:14 – 20.)

5. How did God deliver his people? (See 2 Chronicles 32:20 – 23.)

## Reflection

Hezekiah faced a desperate situation. Jerusalem alone could not defend itself against the mighty Assyrians. Despite the overwhelming odds, Hezekiah trusted God to help his people and protect Jerusalem from the Assyrians.

Imagine yourself in Jerusalem during the time of Hezekiah and the Assyrians. You have heard Sennacherib's insults against the living God. You have heard what he has done to every city in Judah. Only your city, Jerusalem, remains. Does your confidence in God's deliverance remain strong? Why or why not?

As you consider how God saved Jerusalem, what do you learn about him that encourages you to have hope in overcoming the problems you face?

As you think about the challenges you face in life, what outcomes would show that God alone is the true, living God?

Are these the outcomes you want? Why or why not?

If not, what do you need to do in order to better understand what God wants to accomplish through those challenges and in order to get on track with his plans?

When God did his mighty work in delivering Jerusalem from the Assyrians, the people overflowed with gratitude and brought offerings and gifts for the Lord and for Hezekiah. Do you truly have a grateful heart toward the Lord?

In what ways are you holding back your gratitude for the goodness and mercy God has shown to you?

## Memorize

*Hezekiah prayed to the* Lord: *"O* Lord *Almighty, God of Israel, enthroned between the cherubim, you alone are God over all the kingdoms of the earth. You have made heaven and earth. Give ear, O* Lord, *and hear; open your eyes, O* Lord, *and see; listen to all the words Sennacherib has sent to insult the living God. It is true, O* Lord, *that the Assyrian kings have laid waste all these peoples and their lands. They have thrown their gods into the fire and destroyed them, for they were not gods but only wood and stone, fashioned by human hands. Now, O* Lord *our God, deliver us from his hand, so that all kingdoms on earth may know that you alone, O* Lord, *are God."*

*Isaiah 37:15 – 20*

## Day Two | Jesus Displays the Work of God in the Lower City

## The Very Words of God

*The man they call Jesus made some mud and put it on my eyes. He told me to go to Siloam and wash. So I went and washed, and then I could see.*

*John 9:11*

## Bible Discovery

### A Blind Man's Faith

During Jesus' day, most of the common people lived in the Lower City of Jerusalem. They lived simply and, like poor people in many countries today, sometimes found it hard to survive if they were afflicted with disabilities. Jesus often reached out to heal people such as these when he encountered them as he walked through Jerusalem. Notice the impact this one encounter had on various people in Jerusalem.

1.  Jesus was apparently leaving the temple on the Sabbath when he and his disciples saw a blind man. (See John 8:59 – 9:12.)

a. What question about the man's spiritual condition did his disciples ask, and what does it reveal about their beliefs? (See John 9:1 – 2.)

b. What answer did Jesus give, and how would it have challenged what the disciples believed about physical affliction? How does it challenge what you believe about physical affliction? (See John 9:3.)

c. How quickly did the blind man respond to what Jesus told him to do, and what immediate impact did his healing have on people in Jerusalem? (See John 9:6 – 12.)

2. Consider this event in light of the geography of Jerusalem. The temple was at the top of Mount Moriah; the Pool of Siloam was in the Lower City at the far end of the Tyropoeon Valley. Jesus had just left the temple, which was also a likely spot for a person to beg. So it is likely that Jesus put mud on the man's eyes somewhere in the vicinity of the temple. In order to reach the pool of Siloam, the blind man would have had to work his way down many steps.

a. Why do you think Jesus put mud on the man's eyes and then asked him to walk down such a long, difficult path?

b. What does this tell you about the man's faith?

3.  The blind man's healing wasn't the end of the story; he was brought to the Pharisees for questioning. (See John 9:13 – 38.)

    a.  Whose spiritual condition were the Pharisees most concerned about? Do you think they suspected Jesus was the unknown healer? Why or why not? (See John 9:13 – 29.)

    b.  Why were the man's parents afraid of the Jewish leaders, and what does this tell you about the level of tension that was building in Jerusalem related to Jesus? (See John 9:20 – 23.)

    c.  What testimony of faith did the healed man give to the Pharisees in response to their questions and insults? What did that testimony cost him? (See John 9:24 – 34.)

4.  What was the impact of Jesus' second encounter with the healed man? (See John 9:35 – 38.)

    What insight into the character and love of Jesus do you gain from this encounter?

    What do you learn about the blind man's faith and his love for God?

## DATA FILE

### The Districts of Jerusalem

To locate these districts, please refer to the illustration of Jerusalem's Districts on page 145.

### David's City

This was the Jerusalem of David's time, located on a narrow strip of land (Mount Moriah) about ten acres in size; populated by about 1,500 people; naturally defended by the Kidron Valley to the east and the Tyropoeon Valley to the west. Originally named Zion, it received fresh water from the Spring of Gihon.

Events that happened here: Abraham brought Isaac to Mount Moriah to sacrifice him (Genesis 22:1–2,14); the Philistines returned the ark of the covenant (1 Samuel 6:1–2, 12–16); and David purchased the threshing floor of Araunah, which became the site of the temple (2 Samuel 24:18–25); Solomon built the temple on Mount Moriah (2 Chronicles 3:1–2); David was tempted and committed adultery with Bathsheba (2 Samuel 11:2–5); Michal, David's wife, saw him dancing joyfully before the Lord and "despised him" (1 Chronicles 15:27–29).

### Lower City

Home to most of the common people during Jesus' day, it was built on the slope of the Western Hill, reaching into the Tyropoeon Valley. It was where Jesus sent the blind man to wash the mud from his eyes in the Pool of Siloam.

### Upper City

Highest area in Jerusalem (located on the Western Hill and now named Mount Zion), this was the site of Herod's palace and home to wealthy Jews. Probably more Hellenists lived here than lived in the Lower City.

### Business District

Although not named by ancient sources, this district inside the Second Wall held many shops and markets. This was the area Jesus walked through on market day on his way to the cross.

### New City

During and after Jesus' time, the city expanded north. Many wealthy people lived here. Herod Agrippa walled it about thirty or more years after Jesus' crucifixion.

## Reflection

As this story begins, Jesus had just left the Jews who wanted to stone him and put an end to his message. Instead, Jesus turned around and in one simple act made a powerful display of the work of God.

> Read through the story again (John 8:58 – 9:38) and list all of the people who saw the work of God displayed (regardless of how they responded to it) in the blind man's life.

> Try to think of yourself in the blind man's place. Do you think he, a blind beggar, ever imagined himself being a central figure in God's work that would catch the attention of so many other people?

> In what ways does his experience cause you to rethink what God may be doing through the difficult challenges in your life?

Jesus required the blind man to demonstrate faith and obedience, which resulted in his healing.

> In what way(s) does God ask you to demonstrate your faith and obedience when he desires to accomplish his work in your life?

What is your commitment to act in faith even if the way is difficult? (Remember the steps to the Pool of Siloam.)

What can you look forward to when the work of God is accomplished?

## Day Three | Jesus Creates a Stir in the Upper City

### The Very Words of God

> Then the chief priests and the Pharisees called a meeting of the Sanhedrin. "What are we accomplishing?" they asked. "Here is this man performing many miraculous signs. If we let him go on like this, everyone will believe in him, and then the Romans will come and take away both our place and our nation." ... So from that day on they plotted to take his life.
>
> John 11:47 – 48, 53

### Bible Discovery

### *The Religious Leaders Respond to Jesus*

Herod built his palace in the Upper City, which was located on the Western Hill (today called Mount Zion) in the highest section of Jerusalem. The palace, which covered nearly five acres, had beautiful gardens, fountains, and accommodations for hundreds of guests. In the vicinity of the palace are several mansions that are believed to have been the homes of priestly families and wealthy nobility. Although the Romans burned these houses in AD 70, evidence of their splendor remains. They help us to picture the wealth of the Jewish leaders who were greatly threatened by Jesus.

1.  When was the news of the arrival of Jesus, King of the Jews, first heard in Jerusalem's Upper City? (See Matthew 2:1 – 12, 16 – 18.)

    How did the people of that district respond?

    What action did Herod take to preserve his power and position, and do you think he had the support of the Jewish leaders?

2.  After Jesus raised Lazarus from the dead (John 11:38 – 44), what did the chief priests and religious leaders who lived in the mansions of the Upper City do? (See John 11:45 – 57.)

    Why did the members of the Sanhedrin consider Jesus to be such a great threat? (See John 11:47 – 48.)

    What impact did their decision to kill Jesus have on his public ministry at that time, and why do you think Jesus did this? (See John 11:54 – 57.)

3.  Where was Jesus taken for questioning after he was arrested? (See Luke 22:54 – 62; John 18:12 – 18.)

To what part of the city was he most likely taken?

What did Peter, who was Jesus' most boldly obedient disciple, do while Jesus was being questioned? What does his response reveal about the wealth and power of the people who arrested Jesus?

## Reflection

The news of Jesus' birth created shock waves in the world of Herod and the Jewish religious leaders. During Jesus' three-year ministry, his teaching, his life, and the impact he had on people challenged the existing religious and political systems to their core. Understandably, those who were in power reacted as Jesus' teachings and popularity threatened to undermine their power, prestige, and livelihood.

What kinds of people today are threatened by the message of Jesus?

What are they afraid of losing?

In what ways does the message of Jesus undermine what they value?

What of much greater value does Jesus have to offer these people?

How might he want you to bring that message to them?

What in your own life are you so afraid of losing that you, too, seek to silence the message of Jesus? What choice do you need to make?

## Memorize

*Some people, eager for money, have wandered from the faith and pierced themselves with many griefs. But you, man of God, flee from all this, and pursue righteousness, godliness, faith, love, endurance and gentleness. Fight the good fight of the faith. Take hold of the eternal life to which you were called.*

*1 Timothy 6:10–12*

## Day Four | Jesus Fulfills the Scriptures Outside the City Walls

## The Very Words of God

*The high priest carries the blood of animals into the Most Holy Place as a sin offering, but the bodies are burned outside the camp. And so Jesus also suffered outside the city gate to make the people holy through his own blood.*

*Hebrews 13:11–12*

## Bible Discovery

### *Jesus Was Crucified Outside the City Walls*

By going through the Garden Gate, people leaving Jerusalem during Jesus' time could reach the area called the New City — the area where the city was expanding to the north. Although we don't know exactly where the crucifixion took place, the New City was the area to which Jesus was taken. Just outside the gate was an old quarry where people were taken to be stoned, and the Romans crucified people outside of the city along well-traveled routes, such as the way to the New City.

1. After the Jewish leaders decided to have Jesus put to death, to which locations in the city was he taken? Make a list of them and the people involved in each place, then locate as many as you can on the map of Jerusalem's Districts on page 145. (See Matthew 27:1 - 2; 11 - 31; Luke 23:1 - 11.)

2. Where did the soldiers take Jesus to be crucified? Locate these areas on the map of Jerusalem's Districts on page 145. (See Matthew 27:32 - 33, 37 - 40; John 19:16 - 20, 41 - 42.)

3. The fact that Jesus was crucified outside the city walls of Jerusalem is more significant than the customary practice of crucifixion would indicate. In the faith history of the Jewish people, going "outside the camp" (or in this case, the city walls) also has a spiritual significance. As you read the following Scripture passages, notice which activities God designated to happen "outside the camp."

| Scripture Text | What Had to Happen "Outside the Camp" |
|---|---|
| Lev. 16:8–10 | |
| Lev. 16:27 | |
| Lev. 24:13–16 | |
| Num. 5:1–4 | |

## DID YOU KNOW?

The name of the scapegoat, who symbolically carried the Israelites' sins into the wilderness, was derived from the Hebrew word *Azazel*. This word apparently came from the name of the goat-demon who was thought to live in the wilderness.

4. How did the early Christians understand the meaning of Jesus being taken outside the city to be crucified? (See Acts 2:22 - 23; Hebrews 13:11 - 12.)

## Reflection

Think of Jesus walking through Jerusalem's Upper City while he was being interrogated, then walking through Jerusalem's Business District to be crucified. What comments did he hear as he walked, his heart filled with anguish at what was to come? Imagine how his followers felt as they watched him, step by step, heading toward a horrible death on a cross. Yet Jesus was willing to be your "scapegoat," to go outside the city and symbolically carry your sins into the wilderness so that you could come into his kingdom — his holy city.

What is your response to him for what he has done?

No doubt some of the Jewish leaders rejoiced as Jesus was led outside the city walls. Finally they were rid of this troublemaker! Yet the Bible contains no record of Jesus talking back to them, refuting their comments, or defending himself as he walked. What does his example mean to you when you encounter people who mock and persecute you? How do you respond to them?

Few people today, even Christians, take seriously Jesus' example of sacrificial love. It's all too easy to make things "all about us" rather than to love other people so deeply that we pay a high price for that love. In which area(s) of your life might God be calling you to make a sacrifice of love for another person?

# Day Five | Jerusalem: City of the Great King

## The Very Words of God

> I have heard the prayer and plea you have made before me; I have consecrated this temple, which you have built, by putting my Name there forever. My eyes and my heart will always be there.
>
> *1 Kings 9:3*

## Bible Discovery

### *God's Plan for Jerusalem*

Jerusalem had been the focal point of God's dealings with his people for more than a thousand years before Jesus came to earth. God had placed his name and presence in the temple and heard the prayers of those who loved him. God's anger also had burned against his people when they rejected his ways and worshiped pagan gods — often in the same places they had worshiped him. Because of their sin, God removed his people from Jerusalem and sent them to exile in Babylon. But he did not forget his city, and seventy years later his people returned to Jerusalem.

But the tumultuous history of Jerusalem has continued to this day. God's people in Jerusalem have been faithful at some times, unfaithful at others. The temple has been rebuilt and destroyed. Despite all the ups and downs, Jerusalem remains the City of the Great King. It was from Jerusalem that the message of Jesus, the hope of salvation, went out into all the world so that the world would know that God is the one true God.

1. As you read the following excerpts from Jerusalem's history, take note of what nearly led to Jerusalem's destruction, what preserved it, and why.

| Scripture Text | What Nearly Led to Destruction | What Saved the City | Why It Was Saved |
|---|---|---|---|
| 1 Chron. 21:1–6, 14–18 | | | |
| 1 Kings 11:7–13 | | | |

*continued on next page . . .*

| Scripture Text | What Nearly Led to Destruction | What Saved the City | Why It Was Saved |
|---|---|---|---|
| 1 Kings 14:21–24; 2 Chron. 12:1–8, 12 | | | |
| 1 Kings 22:41–43; 2 Chron. 20:2–29 | | | |

2. The day came when the sins of his people grew so great that God would no longer save Jerusalem. (See 2 Kings 21:1 - 7, 12 - 16.)

   a. Why was God so angry that he would not save Jerusalem? (See also 2 Kings 24:3 - 4.)

   b. What was the destruction of Jerusalem by the Babylonians like? (See also 2 Kings 25:1 - 12.)

3. God eventually restored his people to Jerusalem, and it once again became a magnificent City of the Great King. Then he sent Jesus, the Lamb of God, to Jerusalem to save them, but they rejected him and spilled his innocent blood. What did Jesus foresee concerning Jerusalem, and how did it affect him? (See Luke 19:41 - 44.)

How was the Roman destruction of Jerusalem in AD 70 a replay of its destruction by the Babylonians?

4.  Despite long periods when its people were unfaithful to God, what originated in Jerusalem and spread throughout the world? (See Luke 24:45 – 49.)

## Reflection

You have had the opportunity during these two sessions to put yourself in Jerusalem and begin to imagine what it would have been like to live there and experience life in the City of the Great King.

Which events or locations in Jerusalem were particularly meaningful to you? Why?

In what ways have they caused you to reevaluate your relationship with God?

How passionate and uncompromising will you be in following God, or will you choose to follow your own path?

In what ways might you benefit from studying the history of Jerusalem more deeply?

In what way do you better understand the grief Jesus felt when he wept over Jerusalem?

How significant do you think it is that God chose Jerusalem as the place to give his Holy Spirit to the early Christians? As the place from which his name would be preached to all nations?

## Memorize

*The Christ will suffer and rise from the dead on the third day, and repentance and forgiveness of sins will be preached in his name to all nations, beginning at Jerusalem. You are witnesses of these things.*

*Luke 24:46–48*

# THE LAMB OF GOD

After Jesus took his disciples to Caesarea Philippi, where he explained and dramatically illustrated their mission, he turned his attention to fulfilling his mission — his ultimate confrontation against evil. He resolutely focused on the journey toward Jerusalem and the cross that awaited him.

As he went up to Jerusalem from Jericho, he passed through the rugged Judea Wilderness where he had fasted for forty days before Satan had tempted him to abandon God's plan of redemption. He knew that wilderness well. It could have provided an easy refuge, a welcome escape from the horrible death he would soon face. But he didn't disappear into the wilderness. Instead, he stayed on the path that led to the cross.

That path led him directly into Jerusalem and the events of what Christians call Palm Sunday. This video provides the historical, cultural, religious, and political contexts that help us to understand how the Jews viewed what took place that day. This insight makes it evident that Jesus — God's Anointed (*Messiah* in the Hebrew translation) — never proclaimed his messianic identity more clearly, nor displayed the method he would use to bring about his kingdom more pointedly, than during his entry into Jerusalem five days before his death.

For the Jews, Passover was a religious observance and a celebration of their liberation from Egypt. During Jesus' time, it also had become an opportunity to express their longing for political freedom from Rome. In fact, Jews claiming to be "messiahs" had so often caused riots during Passover that the Romans brought extra troops into Jerusalem at that time. They would not hesitate to shed blood to keep the peace.

So what *really* happened as Jesus rode the donkey toward Jerusalem that Sunday before Passover? He came out of the wilderness on the eastern side of the Mount of Olives (as prophecy predicted the Messiah would). Yet he came to the people as the Lamb of God, not as a political deliverer. Jesus, the sinless Messiah who would die on humankind's behalf, presented himself in Jerusalem on the day when each Jewish family selected a "perfect lamb" to sacrifice the following Friday. It's almost as if God was saying, "Here's my Lamb. Will you choose him?"

Instead of turning to Jesus the Lamb, the crowds misunderstood what kind of Messiah he was. Near where the road went down the Mount of Olives, the disciples "began joyfully to praise God in loud voices for all the miracles they had seen" (Luke 19:37). Then the crowd joined in. They spread cloaks and branches on the road before him and began shouting "Hosanna," which meant, "Please save us! Give us freedom! We're sick of these Romans!" They waved palm branches, a symbol that once had been placed on Jewish coins when the nation was free. The branches did not symbolize peace and love, as Christians usually assume; they symbolized Jewish nationalism, an expression of the people's desire for political freedom.

In response, Jesus wept. His tears were not the sorrowful tears of one who feels the pain of a loved one's death. Recently, Jesus had shed those tears at the home of Lazarus, whom he later raised from the dead (John 11:33–35). The tears Jesus shed as people shouted "Hosannas" were tears of grief for his people. Jesus foresaw the terrible devastation of Jerusalem that would result because the people did not recognize him as God's Messiah. They were looking for a Messiah who offered political deliverance and a political kingdom, so they rejected the Messiah who offered deliverance from sin and ushered in God's kingdom by sacrificing his own life.

# Opening Thoughts (4 minutes)

## *The Very Words of God*

> *Rejoice greatly, O Daughter of Zion! Shout, Daughter of Jerusalem! See, your king comes to you, righteous and having salvation, gentle and riding on a donkey, on a colt, the foal of a donkey.*
>
> *Zechariah 9:9*

## Think About It

People who lived during the time of Jesus created their own pictures of who he was just as people do today.

Which words or phrases have you heard people use to describe who Jesus is, and how accurately do they reflect what the Bible says? Why do you think people cling to their own ideas of who Jesus is instead of discovering who the Bible says he is?

# DVD Teaching Notes (20 minutes)

**Jesus' journey toward Jerusalem**

**Jesus' entry into Jerusalem**

**"Lamb day"**

**Passover politics**

**Jesus' tears**

## DVD Discussion (7 minutes)

Refer to the map of the land of Jesus' ministry on page 177. Trace the route Jesus took from Caesarea Philippi through the Decapolis, Perea, across the Jordan, to Jericho and through the Judea Wilderness to Jerusalem.

1.  What did you learn about Jesus' entrance into Jerusalem that was new to you, and how does it help you to understand what happened that day?

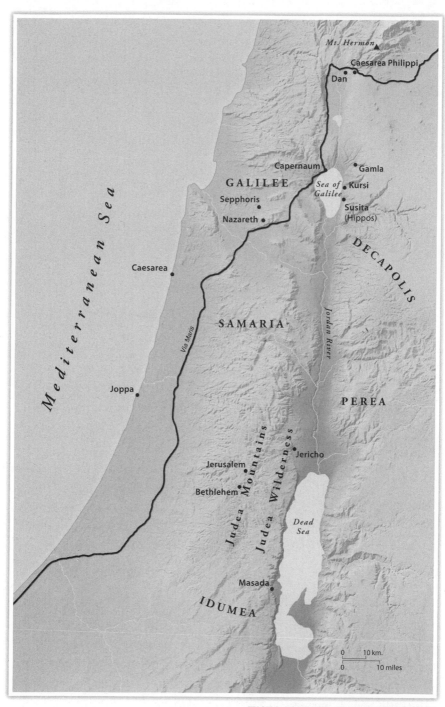

**THE LAND OF JESUS' MINISTRY**

2. Imagine the different people who were in the crowd as Jesus entered Jerusalem. What hopes, expectations, and fears do you think various people in that crowd experienced? Pharisees? Ordinary people? Zealots? Jesus' disciples?

3. The Jews who cried "Hosanna" had an expectation of the Messiah that he could have fulfilled, but did not. Would you say their expectation was wrong, or misapplied? Why?

   What do you think leads people of faith to truly believe that God is doing something he isn't?

   If you feel comfortable doing so, share about a time in your life when you have done this.

## Small Group Bible Discovery and Discussion (18 minutes)

### Jesus Demonstrates His Love

The Bible provides many insights into who Jesus is and how he lived that out while he was on earth. From its pages, for example, we know something of his knowledge of Scripture, how he reached out to different kinds of people and responded to their needs, and his faithfulness to live according to the will of his heavenly Father. Let's take a few minutes to consider the love and compassion Jesus felt and demonstrated toward the people he came to save.

1.  Jesus expressed his love in the tears he shed at Lazarus' tomb. (See John 11:1 – 3, 17, 30 – 44.)

    a.  How well did Jesus know Lazarus? (See John 11:1 – 3.)

    b.  How did Jesus respond to Mary's pain and the pain of other Jews who had come to comfort her? (See John 11:32 – 36.)

    c.  What were Jesus' feelings when he came to the tomb? (See John 11:38.)

2.  Jesus expressed his love in the tears he shed at Jerusalem. (See Luke 18:31 – 33; 19:28, 37 – 44.)

    a.  What did Jesus know would happen to him in Jerusalem? (See Luke 18:31 – 33.)

    b.  How does his determination to travel through the wilderness to get to Jerusalem and face what was ahead add to your understanding of his great love for humanity?

    c.   Why did Jesus weep over Jerusalem? (See Luke 19:37 – 44.)

    d.   How would you describe what Jesus, the Messiah, wanted to do for Jerusalem and its people if they had accepted him as a redeeming Messiah rather than a conquering Messiah?

3.   In everything he did, Jesus demonstrated true love — the pure, perfect, boundless love of God. What do Romans 5:8, Ephesians 5:1 – 2, and 1 John 4:8 – 9 add to your understanding of what true love is?

    How does this picture of love differ from the kind of love we usually see demonstrated in life?

## Faith Lesson (5 minutes)

Although we talk about the love of Jesus, it's not easy for us to understand the depth of love that he demonstrated by coming to Jerusalem to be the sacrificial Lamb for the sins of humanity.

1.   To what extent do the tears Jesus shed for the family and friends of Lazarus and the people of Jerusalem touch your heart and help you to realize the depth of his great love and compassion for people?

2. Which other scenes from the life of Jesus have revealed his love to you and touched your heart and life?

3. Have you recognized Jesus' love for you and accepted him as the perfect Lamb of God, the sacrifice for your sins? If so, what is your commitment of love to him? If not, why not?

4. What can you do to know the loving heart of Jesus more fully and to help other people recognize how Jesus has expressed his love for them?

## Closing (1 minute)

Read together 1 John 4:9 – 10: "This is how God showed his love among us: He sent his one and only Son into the world that we might live through him. This is love: not that we loved God, but that he loved us and sent his Son as an atoning sacrifice for our sins." Then pray, asking God to give you the ability to recognize Jesus as the King he is — not the king you want him to be. Thank him for the compassion he demonstrates to those he loves and invite him to guide you to people who still look for salvation elsewhere.

### Memorize

*This is how God showed his love among us: He sent his one and only Son into the world that we might live through him. This is love: not that we loved God, but that he loved us and sent his Son as an atoning sacrifice for our sins.*

*1 John 4:9 – 10*

# When Following Jesus Is the Most Important Thing in Life

*In-Depth Personal Study Sessions*

## Day One | Jesus Turns His Focus toward Jerusalem

### The Very Words of God

> *Jesus took the Twelve aside and told them, "We are going up to Jerusalem, and everything that is written by the prophets about the Son of Man will be fulfilled. He will be handed over to the Gentiles. They will mock him, insult him, spit on him, flog him and kill him. On the third day he will rise again."*
>
> *Luke 18:31 – 33*

### Bible Discovery

### *Determined to Complete His Work*

As Jesus set his course for Jerusalem, he knew he'd face jeering crowds, betrayal by friends, a Roman cross, and finally the rejection of his own Father while he bore the agony of hell for the very people who despised him. Yet Jesus refused to turn aside from the path before him. Although he could have escaped into the Judea Wilderness at any time as he walked the ten-plus miles between Jericho and Jerusalem, he kept walking toward his destiny. By his faithfulness to God in remaining on the path, he forever changed the eternal future of those who believe in him.

1. The following Scripture texts are in chronological order. As you read them, write out what you discover concerning Jesus' goal and his determination to complete his work.

| Scripture Text | Jesus' Determination to Complete His Work |
| --- | --- |
| Matt. 17:22 | |

| Scripture Text | Jesus' Determination to Complete His Work |
|---|---|
| Luke 9:51 | |
| Matt. 19:1 | |
| Matt. 20:17 – 19 | |
| Luke 10:5 – 7 | |
| Luke 13:22 | |
| Luke 18:31 – 33 | |
| Matt. 20:29 – 30 | |
| Matt. 21:1 | |
| Matt. 21:12 – 16, 23 – 24 | |
| Matt. 26:1 | |
| Matt. 26:10 – 12 | |
| Matt. 26:31 – 32 | |

2. Why was Jesus so determined to go to Jerusalem to die? (See John 12:27 – 28.)

---

**DATA FILE**

**The Judea Wilderness**

*Provided a Place to Hide:*

- David hid from Saul (1 Samuel 23:14).
- Elijah hid from Ahab and Jezebel (1 Kings 19:1 – 5).
- An Egyptian hid from the Roman authorities (Acts 21:38).

*Perceived as a Place of Temptation and Evil:*

- Goat-gods (satyrs) were believed to live in the wilderness (Leviticus 17:7; 2 Chronicles 11:15; Isaiah 13:21).
- Jewish tradition taught that demons, including a fallen angel, lived there (1 Enoch 6 – 13).
- Satan tempted Jesus in the wilderness for forty days (Luke 4:1 – 13).
- Jesus used the wilderness walk between Jerusalem and Jericho as the setting for his parable about the man who was beaten by robbers and left for dead (Luke 10:30 – 37).

---

## Reflection

Today, many of us take "shortcuts" in our relationship with God. Instead of seeking and doing his will, we sometimes choose our own paths. Instead of resolutely following our Shepherd through difficulty or danger, we sometimes take the easier path. Instead of trusting God to guide us along the unknown path, we sometimes choose the path we can see. Yet Jesus followed the difficult path to death even though he saw it clearly.

What does it mean to you that Jesus was so committed to his mission of redemption?

What do you think motivated Jesus to "stay the course" to Jerusalem?

As you think about how faithful and determined Jesus was to complete the mission God had set before him, how do you want to live differently so that you fulfill what God has given you to do? Be specific.

When your path gets rough, which "wilderness escape" do you pursue instead of staying the course and relying on God to help you accomplish his will for you?

What happens to your level of commitment when you know for certain that *God* has established the journey you are taking?

How do you find out if you are on the path God has set in front of you?

## Memorize

*Now my heart is troubled, and what shall I say? "Father, save me from this hour"? No, it was for this very reason I came to this hour. Father, glorify your name!*

John 12:27–28

## Day Two | Jesus Presents Himself as the Messiah — the Lamb of God

## The Very Words of God

*For you know that it was not with perishable things such as silver or gold that you were redeemed from the empty way of life handed down to you from your forefathers, but with the precious blood of Christ, a lamb without blemish or defect. He was chosen before the creation of the world, but was revealed in these last times for your sake. Through him you believe in God, who raised him from the dead and glorified him, and so your faith and hope are in God.*

1 Peter 1:18–21

## Bible Discovery

### Jesus Prepares to Give Up His Life

After Peter confessed that Jesus was the Christ, the Messiah (Matthew 16:13 - 16), Jesus immediately began to teach his disciples about the way in which he would carry out his divine mission. As he, the sacrificial Lamb, journeyed toward the cross, note the ways in which he revealed who he was. Notice the messages his actions sent that indicated how the Old Testament prophecies about the Messiah were being fulfilled.

1. How did the disciples respond to Jesus' direct teaching about his imminent suffering and death? (See Matthew 16:21 - 23; 17:22 - 23.)

Why do you think it was difficult for them to understand even Jesus' direct teaching about the sacrifice he would make?

2. Which principles did Jesus repeatedly seek to communicate to his disciples during this time? (See Matthew 16:24 – 26; 20:17 – 27.)

When do you think they started to understand what this meant for them?

3. What does the Bible say about the disciples' understanding of the kind of Messiah Jesus was and what they expected he would do? (See John 12:12 – 16; Acts 1:4 – 6.)

4. After walking through the Judea Wilderness from Jericho, Jesus reached the Mount of Olives just east of the Temple Mount. From there he proceeded into Jerusalem where the people triumphantly acclaimed him as their king. The following questions will help you to understand the messages Jesus was sending through the manner, timing, and location of his entrance into Jerusalem.

a.  In light of Old Testament prophecy, why was the direction from which Jesus came into Jerusalem significant? (See Isaiah 40:3.)

b.  Jesus entered the city as Messiah on the tenth day of the month when Jewish families picked Passover lambs for sacrifice. What connection was he making between himself and the sacrifice for sin that God required? (See Exodus 12:1 – 6, 12 – 15; Matthew 17:22 – 23; John 1:29; 12:1, 12 – 18.)

    NOTE: Although Western people don't often make connections this way, it is a very Eastern way of thinking. For Jesus, the Messiah, to go into Jerusalem on lamb selection day would have been as obvious a message to people of his day as the link between the terrorist attacks in the United States occurring on 9/11 is to us.

c.  What did Jesus communicate by getting on the donkey in Bethphage — the town the rabbis had decided was the city limit of Jerusalem? (See Zechariah 9:9 – 10; Matthew 21:1 – 7.)

5.  Describe the differences between the way the people responded to Jesus and the way he responded to them. (See Luke 19:37 – 44; John 12:12 – 13.)

## COMPELLING EVIDENCE
### The Messiah from the East

A number of significant events in the history of the Jewish people, particularly events that relate to God's presence, have been recorded as occurring "from the east":

- The children of Israel, with the ark symbolizing God's presence, entered the Promised Land from the east (Joshua 3:1, 15–17).
- In Ezekiel's visions, the glory (presence) of the Lord left the corrupted temple and departed to the east (Ezekiel 10:4, 18–19; 11:22–24).
- Ezekiel saw the glory of the Lord return to the temple from the east (Ezekiel 43:1–5).
- Jesus' birth was announced in the east (Matthew 2:1–2, 9).
- The prophet Isaiah said that the Messiah would come from the wilderness east of Jerusalem (Isaiah 40:3).
- Jesus ascended into heaven from the Mount of Olives, east of Jerusalem (Acts 1:6–12).
- The Mount of Olives, east of Jerusalem, represents Jesus' second coming (Zechariah 14:4; Joel 3:2, 12).

## Reflection

It's not easy to comprehend the selfless sacrifice that Jesus the Messiah *chose* to make for the sake of all humanity. Even the people of his day, for the most part, believed their own concepts of Jesus rather than believing his prophetic words about his imminent sacrifice of death. Yet Jesus came to serve and eventually to suffer and die for the sins of humanity. That was the plan from the beginning (John 12:27).

In light of what Jesus was willing to give for the salvation of the world, how significant is his command to his followers to take up their crosses and follow him?

How eager are you to take up the cross and follow him?

If you are committed to doing that, how important is it that you know Jesus for who he really is, not who you want him to be?

What is your source of information for knowing what kind of Messiah Jesus is, and how well do you know this source?

Jesus knew the Scriptures well. He was faithful and deliberate as he fulfilled the task before him according to the Scriptures. What does the example of his faithfulness reveal to you about how important the Scriptures ought to be to you?

## Day Three | Praised as Messiah, But Not as the Lamb

### The Very Words of God

*On the next Sabbath almost the whole city gathered to hear the word of the Lord. When the Jews saw the crowds, they were filled with jealousy and talked abusively against what Paul was saying. Then Paul and Barnabas answered them boldly: "We had to speak the word of God to you first. Since you reject it and do not consider yourselves worthy of eternal life, we now turn to the Gentiles. For this is what the Lord has commanded us: 'I have made you a light for the Gentiles, that you may bring salvation to the ends of the earth.'"*

*Acts 13:44–47*

## Bible Discovery

### *Desire for a King Overshadows the Gift of the Lamb*

The popular acceptance of Jesus as the Messiah and the rejection of him as the Lamb of God is a tragic irony. It is difficult for people today to understand how deeply and passionately the Jews wanted a saving king. But as we learn how this drama played out in Jerusalem during Jesus' final days, we gain insight not only into the hopes and longings of the ancient Jews for a Messiah king but into our need to recognize anew who Jesus is and why he came to earth.

1. As Jesus taught and performed miracles among the people, some Jews became convinced that he was the promised Messiah. What had the people wanted to do to Jesus during a previous Passover? (See John 6:1 – 15.)

   What had convinced them of this view of Jesus?

   What did Jesus do to prevent them from taking action?

2. Jesus knew what was in the hearts of the people. What did he do the next day to try to open their eyes to the kind of Messiah he was? (See John 6:25 – 27.)

3. What did the crowd do as Jesus rode into Jerusalem? (See Matthew 21:6 – 9; John 12:12 – 13.)

What did the word *Hosanna,* which means "please save," mean in the minds of these people?

4.  Picture what happened next. The crowd shouted, but Jesus wept! Why did Jesus weep when so many people recognized him as Messiah? (See Luke 19:41 – 44.)

    Why didn't Jesus just go away as he had before?

5.  Since Jesus wanted people to recognize him as the Messiah, the Lamb of God, why is it significant that he rode a donkey into Jerusalem on lamb selection day? (See Matthew 21:1 – 7; John 1:29 – 36.)

## Reflection

We are so tuned in to what we want and what we think is good for us that our desires sometimes overshadow our ability to see Jesus for who he really is. How often has God made it clear to us, just as he made it clear to the Jews who wanted to make Jesus king, that what we want is not the most important thing — yet we still don't understand?

God wanted Jesus' identity as the Lamb of God to be clearly revealed to the Jews so that they would profess faith in him as their Messiah. But the people didn't recognize who he was. What happened as a result?

What are some ways in which people today (and we each need to include ourselves) miss seeing who Jesus really is, and who do we see him as instead?

What are the consequences — immediate and big-picture — when we try to make Jesus into someone he isn't, when we fail to recognize him as the Lamb of God who shed his blood to save all humanity from sin?

If you are a Christian, who did you see Jesus to be when you chose to receive him as your Lord and Savior?

Since then, what have you done (and what are you doing) to ensure that you recognize Jesus for who he is?

# Day Four | The Compassionate Heart of Our Savior

## The Very Words of God

*But you, O Lord, are a compassionate and gracious God, slow to anger, abounding in love and faithfulness.*

*Psalm 86:15*

## Bible Discovery

### Jesus Feels Our Pain

When Jesus wept after the death of Lazarus, he knew that he would raise Lazarus from the grave. So why did he cry if Lazarus would live again? And why did he weep over Jerusalem while everyone around him rejoiced? The simple answer is: Jesus loves us. Our God loves us beyond measure. His compassionate heart feels our every pain, whether it is physical, emotional, relational, or spiritual. He weeps for the pain we don't even know is there.

1. Many of the Psalms praise or express hope in God's care for those who experience pain. As you read these portions of the Psalms, take note of how God's love is expressed in terms of his tender, compassionate heart that feels our pain.

| Scripture Text | The Heart of God That Feels My Pain |
|---|---|
| Ps. 23:4 | |
| Ps. 34:18 | |
| Ps. 86:15 | |
| Ps. 103:2 – 4, 13 | |
| Ps. 145:9 | |

2. With these images of God's loving heart in mind, read John 11:33 – 35. What do you realize about Jesus when he wept with the friends and family of Lazarus?

3. How do we know that Jesus feels our pain as deeply as we do? (See Isaiah 53:3 – 5; 2 Corinthians 13:3 – 5.)

What does it mean to you that God is willing for his heart to feel the hurt that you feel? To be crushed, wounded, and afflicted in order to carry your sorrows?

How amazing is it to you that God is willing to comfort you in all of your troubles?

4. What pain does Jesus feel for those who look for hope somewhere other than in him? (See Luke 19:41 – 44.)

How much love does it take to weep for those who reject you?

5. How can we know that God wants to help bear the burden of our pain? (See John 14:27; 1 Peter 5:7.)

## Reflection

God, as Jesus demonstrated while he was on earth, cares deeply for every person — including *you*! In fact, Jesus knows every heartbreak and feels every pain. He weeps with you when you are in sorrow, and he weeps when you misunderstand him and his message. And if you ask, he will provide comfort and peace for you during even the most trying circumstances.

Because of his love and compassion for all he has made, what are some specific things that would cause Jesus to weep? Go ahead, start making a list!

Which specific things cause *you* to weep? Start making a list!

How much are they like or unlike the things that would cause Jesus to weep?

If you want to develop a heart that is more like the compassionate heart of Jesus, try making a daily list of what you have seen and heard that would cause Jesus to weep.

Jesus weeps for Christians' hurts and sorrows like he wept for the family and friends of Lazarus. He also weeps for people who have missed him and his message. Why does Jesus weep for you?

If you are a Christian, to what extent are you receiving Jesus' comfort — and in turn sharing it with other people who are in pain?

## Memorize

> *Come to me, all you who are weary and burdened, and I will give you rest. Take my yoke upon you and learn from me, for I am gentle and humble in heart, and you will find rest for your souls.*

> *Matthew 11:28 – 29*

## Day Five | Our Model for Selfless Sacrifice

### The Very Words of God

> *Even the Son of Man did not come to be served, but to serve, and to give his life as a ransom for many.*

> *Mark 10:45*

### Bible Discovery

### *Jesus Calls Us to Live a Life of Sacrifice*

As would most of us, Jesus' disciples had difficulty understanding that he would accomplish his mission by suffering, serving others, and dying for those who did not deserve it. Through his example,

Jesus challenged his early disciples to follow him as obediently as sheep follow their shepherd. Today he calls us to do the same.

1. The model of self-sacrifice that Jesus established for his disciples didn't come naturally for them, and it doesn't come naturally for us. Look up each of the following Scripture passages and list the characteristics of a life of service that Jesus wanted his disciples to demonstrate. Then write down practical ways in which you can begin living as Jesus lived.

| Scripture Text | A Disciple Who Serves ... | How I Can Begin Living This Way |
|---|---|---|
| Matt. 5:14–16 | | |
| Matt. 5:23–24 | | |
| Matt. 5:43–47 | | |
| Matt. 18:21–35 | | |
| Matt. 20:25–28 | | |
| Matt. 25:31–45 | | |
| John 13:34–35 | | |

2. In contrast to the example of sacrifice that Jesus lived out, what were some of the disciples' concerns? (See Matthew 18:1 - 4; 20:20 - 24.)

3. When Jesus heard what the disciples desired, what did he remind them was most important? (See Matthew 20:25 – 28.)

## FAITH PROFILE
### The "Doubting Thomas" Most of Us Never Knew

Most Christians remember Thomas as the disciple who:

- Didn't believe the other disciples when they told him they'd seen the risen Jesus (John 20:19 – 25).
- Said that he'd only believe if he touched Jesus' scarred hands and side (John 20:25).

But Thomas also demonstrated great faith and dedication to Jesus during the walk to Jerusalem. When Jesus told his disciples that they were returning to Judea, they protested, recalling that the Jews had tried to stone him there (John 11:7 – 8). But Thomas courageously agreed with Jesus, saying, "Let us also go, that we may die with him" (John 11:16). And the disciples remained with Jesus and headed toward Jerusalem.

## Reflection

God calls each of us who would follow the Messiah to live a loving, sacrificial life. He commands us to be kind to enemies, to not judge one another, to be forgiving, to serve others, and above all else to love him with all our heart, soul, and strength. That's quite an opportunity, isn't it?

Why is the life of sacrifice that Jesus lived such an important model for Christians to follow?

What real difference does Jesus' example of sacrifice make in *your* life?

How significant an adjustment is it for people who live in a culture in which everyone wants to be first and to have the best to really understand and follow the Messiah who gave up everything, even his life, for them?

What are some of the changes in thinking, behavior, and attitude that we must make in order to follow his example?

What happens when we become excited about following Jesus but lose our focus on what that will require of us?

How should the fact that Jesus came to serve, and also commanded his disciples to serve sacrificially, influence your thoughts and actions every day?

## Memorize

*Whoever wants to become great among you must be your servant, and whoever wants to be first must be your slave — just as the Son of Man did not come to be served, but to serve, and to give his life as a ransom for many.*

*Matthew 20:26 – 28*

# THE WEIGHT OF THE WORLD

At the time Jesus lived, olives were the most significant crop in Israel. Olives and the oil they produced were used for such everyday purposes as food, lighting, lubrication, and health care. They were also used for ceremonial purposes such as offerings and the anointing of leaders.

Images of the olive tree, its fruit, and its oil are frequently used in the Bible. God used these images to portray himself, his blessing, and his Messiah. So this session will focus on Jesus' final night in Gethsemane on the Mount of Olives before he bore the weight of our sins on the cross. We will also explore other ways in which God used the symbols of olives and olive trees to reveal his message.

To extract olive oil, the Jews used an olive press — a *gethsemane*. They lowered heavy stone slabs onto baskets of olives that had already been crushed in an olive crusher. Gradually the pressure of the slabs' weight squeezed the oil out of the olive pulp, and the oil ran into a pit where it was collected in clay jars.

After the Last Supper, when Jesus washed his disciples' feet, he went to a *gethsemane* — an olive press in or near an olive grove on the Mount of Olives (see Mark 14:32; John 18:1) where his betrayer would be certain to find him. The image of the gethsemane where Jesus went that night before his crucifixion provides a vivid image of the suffering he experienced then. The weight of all humanity's sin pressed down on him in the same way that heavy stone slabs pressed down on olives in an olive press.

Greatly distressed over his imminent suffering, Jesus sought to find strength in prayer — through his own prayers to his Father and through the prayers of those who were closest to him. When his sleeping disciples abandoned him, Jesus openly shared with his Father the deep emotions he felt as he anticipated the dreadful day ahead.

Jesus knew that he had to face the weight of:

- Abandonment by his disciples
- A trial by religious leaders
- Torture at the hands of Roman soldiers
- Crucifixion and physical death
- His Father's rejection as he suffered the agonies of hell to pay for the sins of those he loved — the sins of you and me

As Jesus prayed, the emotional weight of what would be laid on him literally squeezed drops of his blood out of him. His sweat, "like drops of blood falling to the ground" (Luke 22:44), flowed from him like olive oil flowing into the pit of the olive press. His flowing blood was his "anointing" for us (2 Corinthians 1:21). His agony provides a profound picture of God's love, Jesus' humanity, and the awful price that had to be paid for our sin.

## Opening Thoughts (4 minutes)

### The Very Words of God

> *He was pierced for our transgressions, he was crushed for our iniquities; the punishment that brought us peace was upon him, and by his wounds we are healed. We all, like sheep, have gone astray, each of us has turned to his own way; and the LORD has laid on him the iniquity of us all.*
>
> *Isaiah 53:5 – 6*

### Think About It

Sin has an impact we can feel. We may feel guilty, wounded, or fearful because of sin, and we often describe those feelings in physical terms such as being crushed, weighed down, or suffocated.

Which words would you use to describe what sin feels like? In contrast, how would you describe what it feels like to be forgiven?

## DVD Teaching Notes (19 minutes)

**Symbolism of the olives**

**A gethsemane (olive press)**

**The curse**

**The importance of producing fruit**

## DVD Discussion (7 minutes)

1.  Capernaum was home for Jesus during much of his ministry. What did you learn about this town that helps you to better understand Jesus' pronouncement of judgment when its people rejected his message and refused to repent?

2.  What new spiritual insight into the symbolism of the olive tree or its oil did you discover, and what does it mean to you?

3.  Describe Jesus' state of mind before he was arrested in Gethsemane on the Mount of Olives.

    What was the "weight" on him? Why was he so sorrowful?

    As you consider all that was going through Jesus' mind that night, in which ways do you think his mind-set differed from that of his disciples?

## Small Group Bible Discovery and Discussion (18 minutes)

### Jesus Prays in Anguish in Gethsemane

The olive press — the gethsemane — symbolizes the agonizing weight of our sin that Jesus willingly carried when he was crucified. Our sins are like the big stone slabs in the olive press that forced the oil out of the olives. Our guilt and the required penalty for sin were great, but Jesus' love for us and his obedient devotion to his Father's will were greater, so he bore that burden for us. Despite the crushing burden of sorrow, loss, and pain he felt, Jesus submitted completely to his Father's will.

The details of what happened in Gethsemane are revealed by Matthew, Mark, and Luke. Read each of these accounts, then discuss the following questions. (See Matthew 26:36 – 46; Mark 14:32 – 42; Luke 22:39 – 46.)

1. How troubled was Jesus, and what two things did he want his disciples to do? (See Matthew 26:36 – 38, 40 – 41; Mark 14:33 – 34; Luke 22:40, 46.)

   Why would this have been important to Jesus, and how do you think faithful obedience to Jesus at that time would have benefitted his disciples?

2. What was Jesus asking in his prayers, and what do they reveal about his relationship with God the Father? (See Matthew 26:39, 42; Mark 14:35 – 36; Luke 22:42.)

What do these prayers show you about God's love for us, and what does that mean to you?

How do you think Jesus' prayers would have affected his disciples if they had been awake and watchful?

What might have been the consequences of their failure to keep watch and pray?

3.  Which temptations might Jesus have faced that night, and how was he strengthened for what he soon faced? (See Luke 22:43 – 44.)

## DATA FILE

**Gethsemane**—A word derived from two Hebrew words: *gat*, which means "a place for pressing oil (or wine)" and *shemanim*, which means "oils." During Jesus' time, heavy stone slabs were lowered onto baskets of olives that had already been crushed in an olive crusher. Gradually the weight of the slabs squeezed the oil out of the olive pulp, and the oil ran into a pit. There the oil was collected in clay jars.

The image of the gethsemane on the slope of the Mount of Olives where Jesus went the night before his crucifixion provides a vivid picture of Jesus' suffering. The weight of the sins of the world pressed down on him like a heavy slab of rock pressed down on olives in their baskets. His sweat, "like drops of blood falling to the ground" (Luke 22:44), flowed from him like olive oil as it was squeezed out and flowed into the pit of an olive press.

**Olive Crusher**—The large, round stone basin used to crush olives into pulp. Ripe olives were placed into the basin, which also contained a millstone to crush the olives. A donkey, or sometimes people, pushed on a horizontal beam that rolled the millstone around the basin, crushing the olives. An olive crusher was often placed in a cave, where the moderated temperature improved the efficiency of oil production.

**AN OLIVE PRESS**

## Faith Lesson (6 minutes)

Because of his deep love and compassion, Jesus willingly accepted the agonizing burden of our sin and went to the cross alone. He chose to die for our sins so that each of us could live a new life of righteousness.

1. How would your life be different if Jesus had disappeared into the night and never been arrested?

2.  When Jesus prayed in Gethsemane, he affirmed the sovereignty of God the Father. He trusted in the Father's plan to redeem humanity from sin. As he agonized about the path ahead, Jesus set a powerful example of trust and obedience to God.

    a.  Why is it important that we trust our heavenly Father, just as Jesus did, when we face difficult times?

    b.  When have you had to do this, and for what difficult situation do you need to trust God now?

3.  Jesus loves each of us with a love we cannot fully comprehend. What did you learn about Jesus' love for you today?

    As you realize the dreadful burden of sin that Jesus bore for you, how does it change the way you view your sin?

4.  What specific thing will you do this week in grateful response to the love Jesus demonstrated for you when he took your sins on himself?

## Closing (1 minute)

Read together 1 Peter 2:24: "He himself bore our sins in his body on the tree, so that we might die to sins and live for righteousness; by his wounds you have been healed." Then pray, thanking God for giving his Son to bear your sins. Ask him to make you more sensitive to sin and more willing to confess your sin, repent, and walk forward in forgiveness.

### Memorize

*He himself bore our sins in his body on the tree, so that we might die to sins and live for righteousness; by his wounds you have been healed.*

**1 Peter 2:24**

# When Following Jesus Is the Most Important Thing in Life

*In-Depth Personal Study Sessions*

## Day One │ How Quickly We Forget

### The Very Words of God

> *When they had sung a hymn, they went out to the Mount of Olives.*
>
> *Matthew 26:30*

### Bible Discovery

### *What Were They Thinking?*

Jesus had spent three years teaching his disciples how to follow him. They had learned so much, but they often fell short of their calling. That night in Gethsemane, between the Passover meal and when Jesus was arrested, they fell short again. At the moment when attentive, faithful obedience to Jesus was so important, they lost their focus and left him to face his mission alone.

1. Many Bible scholars are certain that as Jesus and his disciples ended their Passover meal together and went to Gethsemane, they sang a collection of lines from the Psalms called the *Hallel* ("Praise"), since that was the custom of Jewish people at that time. As you read the following portions of the Psalms, note the messages of God's love and faithfulness and the promise of salvation.

| Scripture Text | The Messages |
|---|---|
| Ps. 115:1 | |
| Ps. 116:1 – 2 | |

| Scripture Text | The Messages |
|---|---|
| Ps. 116:3–4 | |
| Ps. 116:12–14 | |
| Ps. 118:1 | |
| Ps. 118:5–7 | |
| Ps. 118:13–14 | |

2.  Can you imagine any better encouragement and preparation for the night ahead than for Jesus and his disciples to sing this hymn as they walked to Gethsemane? Why or why not?

    What do you think it meant to Jesus to have this hymn in mind that evening?

    Why do you think its message seems to have been lost on Jesus' disciples?

3.  How had Jesus asked his disciples to follow him that evening, and what was their response? (See Matthew 26:38–45.)

What do you think happened that allowed the disciples to so quickly abandon what was most important even though Jesus was with them?

## Reflection

Every moment of every day we, like the disciples in Gethsemane, must choose how we will respond to God's calling. When difficult challenges come, will we remain focused on where he is leading us to serve him, or will we fall asleep? Will we obey him eagerly and passionately, or will we let down our guard and succumb to temptation? Now would be a good time to think about ways to prepare yourself in order to keep your focus on what is most important.

How important is it to "watch and pray" during times of testing, and how faithful are you in doing this?

When following his calling is difficult, in what ways are you tempted to take your eyes off Jesus?

In what ways do you need to "watch and pray" regarding these specific temptations?

In what way(s) do you relate to Jesus' loneliness as he faced his anguish alone?

When have you faced a lack of support from friends or family members during a crucial time?

How did that lack of support affect you, and what enabled you to continue walking with God?

Who in your life will stand with you and strengthen you when following God's calling is difficult? For whom will you do the same?

In what ways does the hymn Jesus and his disciples sang remind you of what is most important in your walk with God and prepare you to face difficult challenges or sorrow? How can you make this hymn your own?

## Memorize

*Watch and pray so that you will not fall into temptation. The spirit is willing, but the body is weak.*

*Matthew 26:41*

## Day Two | Jesus Shed His Blood for Us

### The Very Words of God

*For God was pleased to have all his fullness dwell in him, and through him to reconcile to himself all things, whether things on earth or things in heaven, by making peace through his blood, shed on the cross.*

*Colossians 1:19 – 20*

### Bible Discovery

### *Jesus Offers a Sacrifice of Love*

Jesus loves people so deeply that he went to the cross alone because his Father said it was the only way to redeem humanity. The aware-ness of this reality led him to such depths of anguish that his sweat became like blood and flowed on our behalf. Our guilt and its pen-alty were great, but Jesus' love for us and his devotion to his Father's will were greater.

1.  What happened to Jesus in Gethsemane as the weight of what he would soon face pressed down on him? (See Luke 22:40 – 45.)

2.  Just hours after his prayers in Gethsemane, Jesus was cru-cified, giving his life and shedding his blood so that all of humanity could be forgiven and reconciled to God. Read the following verses and write out, as a reminder to yourself, what Jesus' shed blood has accomplished (and is accomplish-ing) in your life.

| Scripture Text | What Jesus' Blood Has Done (and Is Doing) for Me |
|---|---|
| Eph. 1:7 – 8 | |

| Scripture Text | What Jesus' Blood Has Done (and Is Doing) for Me |
|---|---|
| Col. 1:19–20 | |
| Heb. 13:12 | |
| 1 John 1:7–10 | |
| Rev. 1:4–6 | |

## Reflection

Today, the eternal hope of all people rests on the blood Jesus shed more than two thousand years ago just outside Jerusalem. What God accomplished there and your response to his offer of salvation plays a crucial role in your life and in the lives of those around you — here and in eternity.

How seriously do you view your sin in light of Jesus' willingness to shed his own blood so that your sins could be forgiven?

What does God's great desire to reconcile every person to himself really mean to you?

In which specific ways do you express your response to what he has done for you? In acts of worship? In faithful obedience?

What freedom does Jesus' shed blood provide?

If you are a Christian, how effectively are you living in light of your freedom from sin?

If you are a Christian, how quickly do you confess your sins to God and repent from your pursuit of sin?

If you are not a Christian, what is keeping you from experiencing God's gift of freedom from sin?

You have been redeemed not only for yourself, but so that all the world will know the one true God. Freedom from the bondage of sin is a gift God wants us to share with others. In what specific ways, and to which individuals, are you revealing the miracle of Jesus' shed blood so that they, too, can be reconciled to him?

## Memorize

*God demonstrates his own love for us in this: While we were still sinners, Christ died for us. Since we have now been justified by his blood, how much more shall we be saved from God's wrath through him!*

*Romans 5:8–9*

## Day Three | A New Perspective on "Little Ones"

### The Very Words of God

> *I tell you the truth, unless you change and become like little children, you will never enter the kingdom of heaven. Therefore, whoever humbles himself like this child is the greatest in the kingdom of heaven.*
>
> *Matthew 18:3 – 4*

### Bible Discovery

#### Adjusting Our View of Who Is Most Important

Jesus was continually adjusting the focus of his disciples — from seeing things as the world sees them to seeing things in light of the kingdom of God. One day he used a little child to help them understand his view of people who seem unimportant in the world's eyes.

1.  What burning question about the kingdom of heaven was on the disciples' hearts? (See Matthew 18:1 - 4; Mark 9:33 - 35.)

    Jesus must have been disappointed by what they were thinking and arguing about, but what was his attitude as he answered them? Would you have answered in this way? Why or why not?

    What did Jesus say was the path to greatness in his kingdom?

    Which specific qualities did Jesus say are necessary?

2.  While the disciples were focused on the child, Jesus taught them two more principles about how those who are unimportant in society are viewed in the kingdom of God.

    a.  How precious are "little ones" in the sight of God, and what does Jesus say will happen to anyone who causes one of them to stumble in their faith? (See Matthew 18:6, 10 – 14; Mark 9:42.)

    b.  How does Jesus look upon anything that is done on behalf of "little ones"? (See Matthew 18:5; 25:34 – 40; Mark 9:36 – 37.)

## Reflection

It may be easier for us to relate to the disciples' treatment of the "little ones" than we would like to admit. Our culture honors accomplishment and pride above service and humility. As we race through life thinking about our own greatness, it's easy to ignore the "little ones" around us.

To what extent had you already understood the severe consequences Jesus pronounced on those who would harm the faith of a "little one"?

What are some of the things we do, even unintentionally, that could harm the faith of a "little one" — a child, a homeless person, a severely disabled person, a poor person, a foreigner, etc.?

In what ways does the strength of his pronouncement cause you to respond differently — in thought, word, and deed — to people who are overlooked and seemingly unimportant in society?

Which "little ones" might you tend to overlook today? What will you do to reach out to them instead of ignoring them?

What needs to change in your heart so that you can approach God in faith like a little child who has nothing to offer versus approaching him on the basis of your own merit?

## Day Four | God's Spirit: Symbolized by Olive Oil

### The Very Words of God

*The LORD is the strength of his people, a fortress of salvation for his anointed one.*

*Psalm 28:8*

### Bible Discovery

### *Anointed by God's Spirit*

It's fascinating to trace the symbolism and use of olive oil in the Bible, particularly the Old Testament. Far from just being a traded commodity, olive oil came to symbolize much more — God's blessings, God's Spirit "being poured out," and the acceptance of God's calling, just to name a few. Even more amazing is the fact that God and his people are symbolized by an olive tree, Jesus is symbolized by an olive shoot, and believers in him are symbolized by olive branches!

1. How valuable a commodity was olive oil considered to be in the world of ancient Israel? (See Deuteronomy 11:13 – 14; 28:49 – 51; 2 Kings 20:13; 2 Chronicles 2:8 – 10.)

2. In what ways did God specify olive oil to be used in the tabernacle and temple? (See Exodus 29:40 – 41; 30:22 – 32; 34:26; Leviticus 24:1 – 4.)

3. Anointing with oil could indicate honor, blessing, God's calling for a specific task, God's equipping with authority, and the pouring out of God's Spirit.

   a. How was oil used in the selection of Israel's kings? (See 1 Samuel 10:1.)

   b. What accompanied David's anointing as king of Israel? (See 1 Samuel 16:11 – 13.)

   c. Who else has been anointed with God's Spirit? (See Isaiah 61:1; Acts 10:37 – 38; 1 John 2:20.)

## JESUS: OUR SOURCE OF LIFE

When an olive tree becomes too old, it stops bearing fruit and is cut down. From the stump, a new branch is cultivated into a new olive tree. Hundreds of years before Jesus came to earth, the prophet Isaiah compared Jesus — the Messiah (the Anointed One) — to a new shoot that will spring out of the unbelieving nation of Israel and revitalize it. When we become Christians, we are in a sense grafted into Jesus — our life-giving branch. We gain our life and energy to bear fruit from him.

### Reflection

The eternal flame of the temple menorah was lit by the oil of olives that were specially prepared for this sacred role. The light of this flame symbolized God's presence that enlightened the world. The olive tree, which produced the oil for anointing, also produced the light that would light the world. It was only natural that Jesus, the Anointed One, would call himself the "light of the world" (John 8:12). It is also not surprising that those who have been anointed by his Spirit should be the light of the world as well (Matthew 5:14).

*Anointing* is not a familiar practice to most contemporary Americans. (We don't anoint our presidents, for example.) From what you have learned through this study, are you anointed? What does being anointed mean to you?

How does the symbolism of being anointed with oil (representing the Holy Spirit) help you to better understand God? Jesus? Your spiritual calling?

How does the fact that God calls (and anoints) every Christian to be the light of the world make a difference in your daily life?

What happens to your "light" if you pull away from God and are no longer being filled with the "oil" of the Holy Spirit?

Do you ask God to "pour out" his Spirit on you? Why or why not?

Think of a Christian you know who is truly being a light where God has placed him or her. What can you learn from that person's example about being God's light where he has placed you?

## Day Five | Bearing the Fruit of Righteousness

### The Very Words of God

*For this reason, since the day we heard about you, we have not stopped praying for you and asking God to fill you with the knowledge of his will through all spiritual wisdom and understanding. And we pray this in order that you may live a life worthy of the Lord and may please him in every way: bearing fruit in every good work, growing in the knowledge of God, being strengthened with all power according to his glorious might so that you may have great endurance and patience, and joyfully giving thanks to the Father, who has qualified you to share in the inheritance of the saints in the kingdom of light.*

*Colossians 1:9 – 12*

## Bible Discovery

### *God's People Are to Bear Fruit*

In the Bible, the olive tree is one of the ways God represents his relationship to his people. In keeping with this metaphor, a Christian's fruitfulness is likened to a tree that bears good fruit. In fact, Jesus strongly condemned unfruitfulness: "A good tree cannot bear bad fruit, and a bad tree cannot bear good fruit. Every tree that does not bear good fruit is cut down and thrown into the fire" (Matthew 7:18 – 19).

1.  Which images are used to describe God's people in Psalm 52:8 – 9 and Hosea 14:5 – 6?

2.  What are the consequences of not bearing good fruit — even for God's chosen and beloved "olive trees"? (See Jeremiah 11:14 – 17; Matthew 3:10 – 12; 7:16 – 20.)

3.  What did God promise to do using the stump of unfaithful Israel? (See Isaiah 11:1 – 3; Jeremiah 23:5 – 6; 33:15 – 16.)

4.  What has Jesus commanded everyone who claims to follow him to do, and what is involved in doing this? (See John 15:12 – 16.)

## DID YOU KNOW?
### The Amazing Olive Tree

- Its roots can live for more than a thousand years.
- An olive tree rarely reaches twenty feet high.
- An olive tree must be cut down when it becomes old (often after hundreds of years) in order to become fruitful again. The next year, new shoots will grow out of the stump, and the tree will produce olives again.
- A good olive tree may produce fifty pounds of olives and four to six pounds of oil each year.
- Olive oil was used for food (1 Kings 17:12), skin care (Ecclesiastes 9:7 – 8), fuel, medicine, and in trade (1 Kings 5:11). It kept leather soft (Isaiah 21:5); priests mixed it with the morning burnt offerings (Exodus 29:40); and it was a symbol of God's Spirit (James 5:14).

## Reflection

It's amazing to think that God — the sovereign Creator of the universe — desires a close relationship with every person he has created! He desires to provide us with everything we need to be "fruitful," so that we will be transformed into the likeness of Jesus the Messiah and be a light to the world.

What things please the Lord and enable us to live as fruitful children of light?

How much of these are a part of your daily life?

What has happened to you when you have tried to grow good fruit on your own, apart from God?

What did you learn through that experience?

Why is God so committed to helping every Christian be "fruitful" and yet so willing to "prune" away our unfruitfulness?

How committed are you to passionately obeying God and allowing him to make you fruitful?

What steps are you taking to become more fruitful and "bear fruit that will last"?

What are you doing to vigilantly examine your life and deal with any unfruitfulness?

## Memorize

*For you were once darkness, but now you are light in the Lord. Live as children of light (for the fruit of the light consists in all goodness, righteousness and truth) and find out what pleases the Lord.*

*Ephesians 5:8 – 10*

# ROLL AWAY THE STONE

Jesus' death and resurrection are the defining events in the New Testament — indeed, in all of Scripture. During this session, you will explore the significance of Jesus' death, burial, and resurrection and what his sacrifice means to Christians today. You will gain a more comprehensive understanding of the great work of love that God accomplished through his son, Jesus.

Because of his love for us, God unleashed his awesome power to accomplish three great works through Jesus' death and resurrection:

- He completed a promise made to Abraham that he would shed his blood for the sins of Abraham and his descendants.

- He made the ultimate sacrifice by offering his sinless life in exchange for ours.

- He offered the cup of salvation — his marriage cup, his life — to us. It is up to us to choose whether we will drink from it and thereby declare that we accept his gift and commit our lives to him.

As a result of what God accomplished during those three days, all of humanity has been given eternal hope. When Jesus the Lamb of God died, the sacrifice for the sins of all humanity was made, providing forgiveness and restoration for everyone who believes. When he rose again, Jesus shouted out to the world that he was who he said he was — the Messiah God had promised through the prophets — and that everything he said was true. Because Jesus lives, the power of God's Spirit indwells every Christian and provides the strength, wisdom, and guidance we need to live for him.

The resurrection proclaimed that God has the power to overcome physical death: no tombstone, no grave, no cross, and no Roman soldier could stop the redemptive work of Jesus Christ. When he rose from the tomb, Jesus showed himself to be the ultimate power over the evil one and his powers. Today, he sits at the right hand of God the Father, interceding for his followers until he comes to earth again.

Although you may be quite familiar with the biblical facts surrounding Jesus' death, burial, and resurrection, this session presents cultural details that heighten their meaning to us:

- Why, for example, Joseph of Arimathea's donation of the hand-hewn tomb was such a great sacrifice. The tomb was brand new and costly, more than a year's wages. It was a gift, not a loan. Once Jesus was buried in the tomb, neither Joseph nor any member of his family could ever use it.

- The significance of Jesus dying at three o'clock on the afternoon of the Passover. Jesus, the perfect Lamb of God, was sacrificed for us. He died at the moment the high priest killed the lamb in the temple that would be offered on behalf of the Jews' sins.

- Why the stone was rolled away from the tomb. The stone was no barrier to Jesus' resurrection. Rather, the stone was removed so that his disciples — and, in a sense, all of humanity — could look in and see that Jesus had risen!

If we truly believe that Jesus is alive today, we must live accordingly. It's not enough to know that Jesus died and was buried. In the same way that those who knew and loved Jesus while he lived on earth saw the empty tomb and believed, we must "look into the tomb" ourselves and affirm: "He is risen! I know that Jesus is alive!" And, just as the angel rolled away the stone in front of the tomb so that

Jesus' disciples could see that he had risen, we must be instruments of God who, in effect, roll the stone away so that other people will see the empty tomb.

## Opening Thoughts (4 minutes)

### The Very Words of God

> *On the first day of the week, very early in the morning, the women took the spices they had prepared and went to the tomb. They found the stone rolled away from the tomb, but when they entered, they did not find the body of the Lord Jesus. While they were wondering about this, suddenly two men in clothes that gleamed like lightning ... said to them, "Why do you look for the living among the dead? He is not here; he has risen!"*
>
> Luke 24:1 – 6

### Think About It

Many people today think of one's faith as being a personal choice with personal impact. They take the position that people can believe in whatever gives them hope and it doesn't really matter to anyone else.

In contrast, how has Jesus' resurrection changed the course of human history and provided hope for all of humanity?

## DVD Teaching Notes (22 minutes)

Blowing of the shofar

**The gift of the tomb**

**The stone rolled away**

**The offering of the cup**

## DVD Discussion (7 minutes)

1. What insights into Jesus' sacrificial death, burial, and resurrection did you gain by watching this video?

   What have those insights helped you to understand or appreciate in a new way?

2. Why was Joseph of Arimathea's gift of the tomb so remarkable?

What do you think inspired such a generous gift, and what do you think it meant to Jesus? (It might help to consider Mary's anointing the feet of Jesus with expensive perfume as you discuss this.)

3. What did the stone being rolled away from the door of the tomb enable Jesus' disciples to do? Why was this important then? Why is it still important?

## Small Group Bible Discovery and Discussion (17 minutes)

### *The Tomb Is Empty!*

It is not enough to know that Jesus was buried: he had to live again in order to defeat the power of Satan. Jesus' resurrection proclaimed God's power over everything — Roman soldiers, the cross, physical death, and the powers of evil. That is why it is so important for us, in effect, to look into the tomb for ourselves and say, "I know Jesus is alive!"

1. Despite all the times Jesus had told his disciples that he would die and rise again, they never seemed to realize that it would actually happen. In what specific ways had Jesus

alluded to, taught, and warned of his upcoming death, burial, and resurrection?

| Scripture Text | How Jesus Tried to Tell Them He Would Die |
| --- | --- |
| Matt. 12:40 | |
| Matt. 26:31–32 | |
| Mark 8:31 | |
| Mark 9:9 | |
| Mark 9:30–31 | |
| John 2:18–19 | |

Why do you think people, especially his disciples, didn't "get" it?

Why is it hard for many of us to understand that Jesus had to die and rise again to redeem us from sin?

2. Although Jesus had tried to help his followers understand what would happen to him, the morning of the resurrection was a startling revelation.

a. When the stone was rolled away from the tomb, what happened to the Roman guards? (See Matthew 27:62 – 28:4.)

b. How did the women respond when they saw the angel and the empty tomb and realized what had happened? (See Matthew 28:1 – 8.)

c. How did the disciples respond when they heard the news? (See Luke 24:9 – 12.)

d. Why was it necessary for Jesus' followers to see the empty tomb?

## Faith Lesson (4 minutes)

When the angel rolled the stone away from the entrance to Jesus' tomb, the disciples could go inside and see that Jesus was not there. The empty tomb was a stunning realization — even the disciple Peter, who always had something to say, was baffled (Luke 24:12). Jesus soon appeared to those who knew him — alive, just as he had promised. To know that the tomb is empty and that Jesus is alive is still a remarkable truth.

1. If you could go back in time and see Jesus' empty tomb with your own eyes, what difference would it make to you?

   What does your answer reveal about what you truly believe?

2. If you believe that Jesus is alive — that the tomb was indeed empty — what difference should it make in your life today? In how you live? In your commitment to serve him? In what you tell others?

3. The impact of the empty tomb is no less stunning today than it was two thousand years ago. The angel rolled the stone away from Jesus' tomb so his disciples could see that he had risen. What can you do to invite people to look inside the empty tomb and, in effect, see for themselves what God has done?

## Closing (1 minute)

Read together 1 Peter 1:3 - 4, "Praise be to the God and Father of our Lord Jesus Christ! In his great mercy he has given us new birth into a living hope through the resurrection of Jesus Christ from the dead, and into an inheritance that can never perish, spoil or fade — kept in heaven for you." Then pray, thanking God for the great work he has accomplished for you through Jesus' death and resurrection. Ask for the courage to stand up and proclaim what God has done so that others can see that the tomb is empty.

## Memorize

*Praise be to the God and Father of our Lord Jesus Christ! In his great mercy he has given us new birth into a living hope through the resurrection of Jesus Christ from the dead, and into an inheritance that can never perish, spoil or fade — kept in heaven for you.*

*1 Peter 1:3 – 4*

# When Following Jesus Is the Most Important Thing in Life

*In-Depth Personal Study Sessions*

## Day One | It Happened According to the Scriptures

### The Very Words of God

> He said to them, "This is what I told you while I was still with you: Everything must be fulfilled that is written about me in the Law of Moses, the Prophets and the Psalms." Then he opened their minds so they could understand the Scriptures. He told them, "This is what is written: The Christ will suffer and rise from the dead on the third day, and repentance and forgiveness of sins will be preached in his name to all nations, beginning at Jerusalem. You are witnesses of these things."
>
> *Luke 24:44–48*

### Bible Discovery

### *The Scriptures Were Written to Help Us Understand*

The Bible is a continuous story, the story of God's redeeming work in human history and in individual people. So it's not surprising that Jesus' suffering and crucifixion had been described many years before those events occurred. What was written by the prophets was there to help the people of Jesus' day understand his life and work, and it is still there to help people understand what God has done.

1.  Read the prophecies in the Old Testament texts on page 237 and take note of what was written. Then compare what was predicted to the actual events surrounding Jesus' crucifixion as recorded in the Gospels. Record your study in the chart.

| Prophetic Text | What the Text Predicted | What Actually Happened |
|---|---|---|
| Isa. 53:7<br>Mark 14:60–61;<br>15:3–5 | | |
| Ps. 22:16–18<br>Mark 15:25–32;<br>John 19:23–24 | | |
| Ps. 34:20; Zech. 12:10<br>John 19:31–37;<br>20:10–11 | | |
| Ps. 69:21<br>Matt. 27:48 | | |
| Isa. 53:3<br>Matt. 26:65–67;<br>27:39–40; John<br>19:14–15 | | |

2. Jesus was, of course, rejected by those who wanted him to be crucified. But Jesus was also misunderstood and rejected by those who followed him. As you read the passages below and on page 238, note who rejected Jesus and why. Imagine how Jesus suffered when each of these turned away and left him to face his ordeal alone.

   John 6:66

John 7:47 – 53

Matthew 26:14 – 16

Matthew 26:56

Matthew 26:69 – 75

Matthew 27:46

## Reflection

After all that had been written about the coming Messiah, and after all that the Jews had done to know the Scriptures and to seek him, most of them didn't connect the message with the person. Even after his resurrection, when Jesus met some of his own disciples on the road, they did not recognize him (Luke 24:25). In response he exclaimed, "How foolish you are, and how slow of heart to believe all that the prophets have spoken! Did not the Christ have to suffer these things and then enter his glory?" May we be diligent in seeking to *understand* all that the Scriptures teach us.

What role do prophecies such as the ones written about Jesus play in helping you to recognize and understand the truth of the inspired Word of God and its relevance to your life?

For what reason(s) do you think many of Jesus' disciples, who knew Scripture well, didn't seem to "connect the dots" linking these Old Testament prophecies to Jesus and his suffering and crucifixion?

What do you do when you read something in the Scriptures that you do not understand?

In light of how important it is to understand the Scriptures, what additional things will you commit to do in order to learn them, understand them, and connect them to what is happening in your life and your world?

## Memorize

*You diligently study the Scriptures because you think that by them you possess eternal life. These are the Scriptures that testify about me, yet you refuse to come to me to have life.*

*John 5:39 – 40*

## COMPELLING EVIDENCE

There is an abundance of evidence in Scripture and in the religious practices of the Jews that God carefully planned the timing of Jesus' death and resurrection. The following are just a few examples of God's planning:

- Prophecies given hundreds of years before Jesus was even born were precisely fulfilled when he died.
- The high priest's practice of killing the Passover lamb had been in force for centuries. On Friday of the year Jesus died, the Jews celebrated Passover and killed a lamb for the temple sacrifice. Jesus, the Lamb of God, died at that same time in order to take our sins upon himself.
- The year that Jesus died, Saturday — the Sabbath — was also the day on which the Jews celebrated the Feast of Unleavened Bread. This feast reminded the Jews of the bread that God provided for the Israelites when they left Egypt. Consider the significant parallels between this feast and Jesus' death:

| | |
|---|---|
| Wheat seeds must die in order to bring forth their crop. | Jesus had to die and be buried in order to accomplish his ministry and be raised to new life. |
| Unleavened bread was made without yeast because yeast represented sin (1 Corinthians 5:7 – 8). | Jesus, the Lamb of God, was sinless. |

- On the Sunday following Jesus' death, the Israelites celebrated the Feast of Firstfruits, which in this case celebrated the beginning of the barley harvest. The Israelites returned to God the "first part" of everything they had been given to indicate their thankfulness for the harvest, their acknowledgment that God had given them the gifts, and their faith that he would continue to provide (Numbers 15:17 – 21; Deuteronomy 26:1 – 11). They gave the best first part of what they received to God (Exodus 23:19). Also, on that day Jesus came to life as God's Firstfruits — the guarantee that the rest would follow — including the resurrection of the dead (1 Corinthians 15:20 – 23).

# **Day Two** | Jesus, the Sacrificial Lamb

## The Very Words of God

> *You are worthy to take the scroll and to open its seals, because you were*
> *slain, and with your blood you purchased men for God from every tribe*
> *and language and people and nation.*
>
> *Revelation 5:9*

## Bible Discovery

### *Jesus Died as the Sacrifice for Our Sins*

As part of his planning, God linked Jesus' sacrifice for all of humanity — every tribe, language, people, and nation — to the annual Passover sacrifice made by the high priest for the sins of the Jews. The
timing of Jesus' death was precise, not circumstantial, and its meaning would not have been lost on his followers. Understanding some
details of the Passover will help us to grasp this amazing truth, too.

1.  Under which circumstances did the first Passover take place,
    and when was it supposed to be celebrated thereafter? (See
    Exodus 12:1 – 14; Leviticus 23:5.)

2.  What does the timing of Jesus' death as the Passover lamb
    was being sacrificed in the temple say about God's plan-
    ning? (See Matthew 27:45 – 50; Mark 15:25, 33 – 37; Luke
    23:44 – 46.)

3. People at the time of Jesus who believed that he was the Messiah recognized his role as the sacrificial Lamb of God.

   a. Early in Jesus' ministry, what did John the Baptist say about him? (See John 1:29 – 34.)

   b. Which words did Paul use to describe Jesus? (See 1 Corinthians 5:7.)

   c. In Hebrews 9:11 – 15, what do we learn about the importance of Christ's sacrificial death?

4. Why is the blood of Christ as important today as it was when he died on the cross? (See 1 John 1:7.)

## JESUS, THE LAMB OF THE WORLD

During Old Testament times, perhaps even going back as far as Moses, the Jewish priests traditionally slaughtered the Passover sacrifice at three o'clock in the afternoon after blowing a shofar — a special horn. They then offered the sacrifice at 3:30, following the daily sacrifice. Both the daily sacrifice and the Passover sacrifice were offered to symbolically cleanse the nation Israel of its sin.

At exactly three o'clock (the "ninth hour" as the Bible puts it in Luke 23:44 – 46), just as the Passover lamb was being killed, Jesus looked up into heaven and said, "Father, into your hands I commit my spirit."

## Reflection

Knowing exactly what would be required of him, Jesus stayed the course, walked the path to the cross, and made himself the sacrifice for the sins of the world. Just as the blood of a lamb on the door-frame caused the angel of death to pass over the homes of God's faithful in Egypt, the blood of the Lamb of God breaks the power of sin and death for those who believe on the name of Jesus.

Today few people fully grasp the concept of blood sacrifices being offered for sin. How deeply must Jesus love you for him to willingly offer himself to pay the price for your salvation?

What has been your response to that love, and in what ways might you want to respond differently?

What difference does Jesus' sacrifice make in your life from day to day and from moment to moment, and how might you want that to change?

Many Christians today know little or nothing about the Old Testament. In what ways has discovering the connections between events in the Old Testament and those in the New Testament helped you to understand more fully what Jesus has done for you?

How important and relevant do you think further study of the Old Testament is for you as you seek to walk with Jesus in your daily life?

When you think of people in your life who do not know Jesus, how might they think differently about him if they realized what he really did for them on the cross?

How might you share this with them?

## Memorize

*God was pleased to have all his fullness dwell in him, and through him to reconcile to himself all things, whether things on earth or things in heaven, by making peace through his blood, shed on the cross.*

*Colossians 1:19–20*

## Day Three | Jesus Is Placed in the Tomb

### The Very Words of God

*Joseph of Arimathea, a prominent member of the Council, who was himself waiting for the kingdom of God, went boldly to Pilate and asked for Jesus' body. Pilate was surprised to hear that he was already dead. Summoning the centurion, he asked him if Jesus had already died. When he learned from the centurion that it was so, he gave the body to Joseph. So Joseph bought some linen cloth, took down the body, wrapped it in the linen, and placed it in a tomb.*

*Mark 15:43–46*

### Bible Discovery

### *What Was the Tomb Really Like?*

Today people still marvel at the ancient tombs in Israel — how they were built, their size, their importance to the people of that day, and the religious laws regarding burial. Although no one knows for sure the exact tomb in which Jesus was buried, we do know certain key details that add insight into the miraculous event of Jesus' resurrection.

1. After Jesus died, who came to claim the body and where did he put it? (Read Matthew 27:57 – 61; Mark 15:43 – 47.)

2. How often had the tomb been used? (See Luke 23:50 – 53.)

3. What was near the tomb? (See John 19:38 – 42.)

4. Of what material was the tomb made, and how was the doorway sealed? (See Matthew 27:59 – 60; Mark 16:4.)

5. What was the door like, and how large was the tomb? (See Mark 16:1 – 5; Luke 24:1 – 4, 12.)

6. According to John 20:1 – 8, what could people outside the tomb see?

## Reflection

Joseph of Arimathea — a wealthy public figure — went against the tide of other members of the Jewish Council and expressed love for Jesus by boldly asking Pilate for Jesus' body. At great personal expense (the tomb would cost about a year's wages), he placed the body of Jesus in his own new tomb.

Joseph of Arimathea's gift of a tomb for Jesus' body was a great sacrifice, even for a wealthy man, so it expressed deep devotion. What would be a way for you to demonstrate a similar level of sacrificial devotion to Jesus?

Would you be willing to do this? Why or why not?

Joseph of Arimathea also spoke out for Jesus in a public setting. When have you spoken out for Jesus in a setting where doing so would be unpopular?

In what way(s) are you willing to stand against the tide of your friends? Your family? The culture in which you live?

Where do you think Joseph of Arimathea obtained the love of heart and strength of will to talk with Pilate about Jesus' body and then give up his expensive tomb?

What have you learned from his example about sharing generously with God's people?

To what extent have you been aware that your actions on behalf of God's people might be affecting people you don't even know, and what does it prompt you to do?

## DID YOU KNOW?

The tomb in which Jesus was placed was brand new. It was located near a garden and belonged to a rich man named Joseph of Arimathea, a prominent member of the Jewish Council.

According to Jewish law held by the Pharisees, only people in an immediate family could be buried in the same tomb, so no one in the family of Joseph of Arimathea could ever use it again.

The tomb was cut from rock and sealed with a large stone. Although the tomb had a low doorway, it was large enough inside to hold more than one person. Often the stone for this type of tomb weighed more than two tons and was rolled across the opening of the tomb.

**A TYPICAL FIRST-CENTURY FAMILY TOMB**

# Day Four | The Temple Curtain Tears in Two

## The Very Words of God

*And when Jesus had cried out again in a loud voice, he gave up his spirit. At that moment the curtain of the temple was torn in two from top to bottom.*

*Matthew 27:50–51*

## Bible Discovery

### By His Blood Jesus Entered the Most Holy Place

For centuries, the Day of Atonement provided the means by which God forgave the sins of his people. In the most sacred place where God's presence lived — the Holy of Holies — only the high priest, and only on that day, was allowed and required to make this essential blood sacrifice. By the power of his own shed blood, Jesus himself entered the presence of God and obtained our eternal redemption.

1. Where did God make his presence known to the people of Israel, and why did it have to be separate from the rest of the temple? (See Exodus 26:31 – 34; Leviticus 16:1 – 2; Hebrews 9:1 – 4.)

2. Who was the only person who could enter the inner room behind the curtain, and how often was he allowed to do it? (See Leviticus 16:29 – 34; Hebrews 9:7.)

3. Why did the high priest offer a blood offering on the Day of Atonement, and what did it accomplish? (See Hebrews 9:7 – 10.)

4. What did the blood of Jesus — the unblemished Lamb of God — accomplish that made the temple curtain obsolete? (See Matthew 27:50 – 51; Hebrews 9:11 – 15.)

## Reflection

Long before Jesus shed his blood as a sacrifice for sin, God had established the Day of Atonement as a special day of sacrifice to cover his people's sins. Every year, the high priest (and only the high priest) approached the presence of God to make this sin sacrifice. The blood of Jesus, however, purchased *eternal redemption* for us — a one-time payment for the sins of the whole world.

In what ways does what you have learned about the Day of Atonement help you to understand why what Jesus accomplished is so important — for you, and for every person who will ever live?

How did Jesus' death and resurrection affect your access to the very presence of God?

In what ways does the fact that you can now approach God directly, rather than having a priest do that for you once a year in the Holy of Holies, influence your relationship with God?

Does it lead you to take your sin more seriously or less seriously than if you (and other people) still had to offer animal sacrifices for sin?

Do you welcome and frequently use the opportunity you have to approach God directly? If yes, why is it so important to you? If no, why don't you value it?

## Memorize

*When Christ came as high priest of the good things that are already here, he went through the greater and more perfect tabernacle that is not man-made, that is to say, not a part of this creation. He did not enter by means of the blood of goats and calves; but he entered the Most Holy Place once for all by his own blood, having obtained eternal redemption.*

*Hebrews 9:11 – 12*

## Day Five | Jesus Offers the Cup of Salvation

## The Very Words of God

*Then he took the cup, gave thanks and offered it to them, saying, "Drink from it, all of you. This is my blood of the covenant, which is poured out for many for the forgiveness of sins."*

*Matthew 26:27 – 28*

## Bible Discovery

### *Accepting the Life Jesus Offers*

During the time of Jesus, it was customary for a couple to seal their engagement by offering and accepting a cup of wine. The prospective groom offered his life, represented by the cup of wine, to the prospective bride. If she accepted the cup from him, it indicated her lifelong commitment to him.

1. To whom did Jesus compare himself? (See Mark 2:18 – 19.)

2. In light of what you learned from watching the video, what was the significance of Jesus offering the third cup of salvation to his disciples during the Passover celebration in the upper room? (See Luke 22:20.)

3. In Revelation 19:6 – 8, what do the "Lamb" and his "bride" symbolize?

   If Jesus is the bridegroom who has already given his life for us, what is our responsibility if we accept his offer?

   In light of the symbolism of the cup, what are we, in effect, saying to God when we drink the cup during Communion?

## DATA FILE

### The Symbolism of the Cup

#### *The Marriage Cup*

During biblical times, a young man who wanted to marry would accompany his father to the chosen woman's house, where she and her father would be present. They'd negotiate a steep "bride price"—the money or physical items that the woman's father would ask for in exchange for giving up his valuable daughter.

Apparently there was a first-century custom that the young man's father would then hand his son a cup of wine. The son, in turn, would offer it to the woman as a way of saying, "I love you, and I offer you my life. Will you marry me?" If she drank it (sealing their engagement), she accepted his life and gave him hers. If not, she simply declined.

#### *The Passover Cup*

There was a custom in Jesus' day that during the Passover liturgy participants would drink from four cups of wine. The third cup was called the cup of salvation. While celebrating the Passover with his disciples in the upper room, Jesus offered them the cup of salvation and said, "This cup is the new covenant in my blood." One of the images he conveyed by these words was, in effect, "I love you. I give you my life. Will you marry me? Will you be my spiritual bride? Will you give your life to me?"

So, every time we drink from the Communion cup when the minister says, "This cup is the new covenant in my blood," God is also saying to us, "I love you. I invite you to be my spiritual bride." And every time we drink it, we are in effect saying to him, "I accept your gift, and I give you my life in return."

#### *The Cup from Which Jesus Drank in Order to Become Our Spiritual Husband*

The night before he died, Jesus asked his Father, "If it is possible, may this cup be taken from me" (Matthew 26:39). He knew the high price he would have to pay to purchase his bride (the church) and become the spiritual husband of every believer.

## Reflection

The church, the bride of Christ, comprises every believer who has accepted the cup of salvation that Jesus offers. Jesus made the ultimate sacrifice for us by offering up his sinless life. As we learn and realize how much Jesus sacrificed for his bride we gain a more complete picture of the depth of his love for each of us and the extent to which we are called to give our lives to him if we accept the cup of salvation.

In what way(s) has Jesus proven his love to you, and what does his love mean to you?

Have you accepted his gift of salvation?

If not, how has what you have learned through this study caused you to reconsider your decision?

If you have accepted his offer, how does the high price Jesus paid to redeem you influence your commitment to him?

Have you fully given him your life in return?

If not, what must you change in order to faithfully live out your commitment to Jesus?

What do you do every day to show Jesus, your spiritual husband, how much you love him?

As you end this study, remember the song at the end of the video. Use it as a prayerful meditation on what Jesus has accomplished for you through his death and resurrection:

> *How beautiful the hands that served,*
> *The wine and the bread and the sons of the earth.*
> *How beautiful the feet that walked,*
> *The long dusty road and the hill to the cross.*
>
> *How beautiful the heart that bled,*
> *That took all my sin and bore it instead.*
>
> *And as he lay down his life,*
> *We offer this sacrifice,*
> *That we will live just as he died.*
> *Willing to pay the price.*
> *Willing to pay the price.*
>
> *How beautiful the radiant bride,*
> *Who waits for her groom with his light in her eyes . . .*
> *How beautiful, how beautiful, how beautiful*
> *Is the body of Christ.*

# POWER TO THE PEOPLE

Following his resurrection, Jesus taught his disciples about the kingdom of God. On the fortieth day, he took his disciples up to the Mount of Olives. There he promised that they would receive power and become his witnesses to the world. Then the disciples watched in awe as Jesus was caught up in a cloud and ascended to his Father in heaven (Acts 1:3 – 12).

As the disciples watched, two men in shining white appeared and promised that Jesus would someday come back in the same way he had disappeared. So the ecstatic disciples returned to Jerusalem to await the baptism Jesus had promised. For ten days they prayed and praised God in the temple. They had little idea of the dramatic transfer of God's indwelling power that would soon take place.

Meanwhile, all around them, the entire Jewish world waited and rejoiced. This was the time of *Shavuot,* one of three annual feasts celebrated in Jerusalem — Passover (*Pesach*), Tabernacles (*Sukkot*), and Pentecost (*Shavuot*) — in which every Jewish male was required to participate. More than a million Jews from all parts of the world were streaming into the city to celebrate and worship in the magnificent marble temple. The city was filled to capacity, and throngs of celebrants filled the streets.

Suddenly, at about 9:00 a.m., during the temple service of Pentecost, a sound like the blowing of a violent wind came from heaven and filled the house where the disciples were. The disciples were filled with the Holy Spirit. Tongues of fire seemed to rest on each of them, and they spoke in other languages. Immediately, bewildered people "from every nation under heaven" gathered around them (Acts 2:5). The people marveled that they could understand the disciples. Although some people mocked, about three thousand others believed and were baptized.

It is likely that this event occurred in the immediate vicinity of the temple — the "house" of God — perhaps on the Southern Stairs, the huge staircase over which hundreds of thousands of Jewish pilgrims made their way to the main processional entrance of the temple. Built by Herod the Great, this unusual staircase had steps of varying widths and was an ideal location for rabbis to teach their disciples. Near the stairs were *mikvoth,* or ritual baths, where Jewish pilgrims purified themselves before worship. These baths may well have been where the three thousand new Christian believers were baptized that day.

On the day of Pentecost, God gave his power to his people. The Holy Spirit, who had filled the temple for so many years, moved into a new temple — the "temple" of individual Christian believers. God was demonstrating that he was beginning a new age, an age rooted in his people — people like you and me who have invited Christ into our lives and allow his Spirit to fill us and empower us to do his will.

## Opening Thoughts (4 minutes)

### The Very Words of God

> You will receive power when the Holy Spirit comes on you; and you will be my witnesses in Jerusalem, and in all Judea and Samaria, and to the ends of the earth.
>
> Acts 1:8

### Think About It

When we face what seem to be insurmountable challenges, we all count on something or someone to encourage and/or strengthen us to do what lies ahead.

What gives a Christian the courage and strength to press on and accomplish the work of God, and what does the visible evidence of that power within the person look like?

## DVD Teaching Notes (17 minutes)

### The Southern Stairs on Pentecost (Shavuot)

### After Jesus' ascension, the disciples wait

### The promised gift of God comes

### What did it all mean?

## DVD Discussion (7 minutes)

1.  On the map of Jerusalem's Districts (page 259), locate the temple and the Southern Stairs. Also note the Mount of Olives east of the temple, from which Jesus ascended to heaven, and the Royal Stoa adjacent to the temple courts where Jesus and the early Christians were known to gather and teach. Imagine bustling crowds of people filling the whole city and thousands upon thousands of worshipers entering the temple on Pentecost morning to celebrate a festival they had celebrated for more than 1,200 years!

    a.  How is your understanding of God's work at Pentecost impacted by the possibility that the "house" the disciples gathered in that morning was in fact the temple?

    b.  Why do you think the Southern Stairs are, or are not, a reasonable place for the disciples to have been on Pentecost morning?

2.  How do you think the disciples felt when they found themselves filled with the Holy Spirit and realized that God's power — the power they had seen Jesus demonstrate time and again, the power he had promised to send — was within them?

A David's City
B New City
C Upper City
D Business District
E Temple Mount
F Lower City
G Herod's Palace

1 Eastern Gate
2 Southern Gate
3 Royal Stoa
4 Robinson's Arch
5 Wilson's Arch
6 Tyropoeon Street
7 Warren's Gate
8 Antonia
9 Tadi Gate
10 Pool of Bethesda
11 First Wall
12 Second Wall
13 Garden Gate
14 Towers
15 (Damascus) Gate
16 Garden Tomb
17 Spring of Gihon
18 Hinnom Valley
19 Theatre
20 Citadel and Herod's palace
21 Essence Quarter
22 Mansions
23 Mount of Olives
24 Kidron Valley
25 Huldah Gates

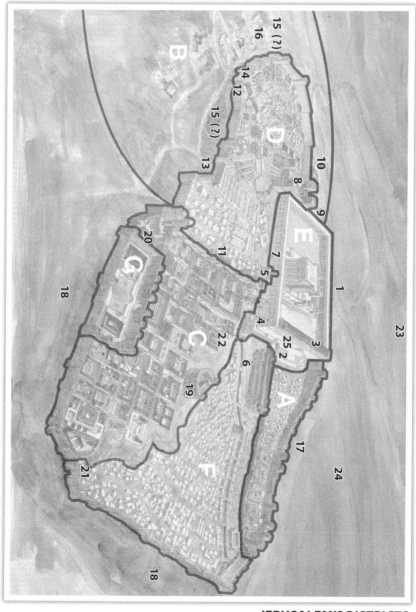

**JERUSALEM'S DISTRICTS**

3. What were the signs that the disciples truly had received the Holy Spirit?

## Small Group Bible Discovery and Discussion (20 minutes)

### When the Church Was Born

After his resurrection, Jesus continued to teach his disciples and prepare them to carry on the work of sharing the news of the kingdom of God. Before he ascended to heaven, Jesus told them that they would become his witnesses beginning in Jerusalem and then to the farthest ends of the earth (Acts 1:8). The prospect of taking his news into the whole world, far beyond Jerusalem and far beyond the realm of those who believed in the God of the Jews, was a daunting task. How could they do it?

1. Just before Jesus ascended to heaven, what did he tell the disciples to do? (See Luke 24:44 – 53.)

   What did they immediately do, and what was their attitude?

   To what extent do you think they knew what they were waiting for and understood what "receiving power from on high" would entail?

2. There was nothing secretive or subtle about the way in which the Holy Spirit came upon Jesus' disciples! (See Acts 2:1 – 12.)

   a. What were the signs that God's power had come upon the disciples? (See Acts 2:1 – 4.)

   b. What caused the loud sound in "the house," and of what did it remind the people who heard it? (See Ezekiel 37:9 – 14; John 3:5 – 8.)

   c. Why were the Jews who had come from many lands bewildered by these events? (See Acts 2:5 – 12.)

3. *Shavuot* celebrated the firstfruits of the grain harvest. Consider the ways the events of Pentecost fulfilled *Shavuot*.

   a. What harvest had Jesus sent his disciples out to gather? (See Matthew 9:37 – 38; Luke 10:1 – 3; John 4:34 – 38.)

   b. What "firstfruits" of the harvest that Jesus had sent his disciples to reap were evident as a result of Peter's preaching? (See Acts 2:14 – 16, 36 – 41.)

4. Why was it important in God's plan that Jews from every nation, who knew their Scriptures and the ways of God, become followers of Jesus the Messiah, the firstfruits of the church?

## Faith Lesson (6 minutes)

As Christians, we are to be to our world what the temple of the Lord was to the world of the Old Testament. We are to reflect God's indwelling presence and make him known. Think about how the early Christians, who for the most part were well versed in the practices and meaning of temple worship, understood the implications of this calling in terms of practical, day-to-day living. Consider, too, what it produced in their lives.

1. At Pentecost, God empowered his disciples to be his witnesses, and they testified to the resurrection of the Lord Jesus with great power. For what reason does God empower his people today?

   Has God empowered you to be his witness? How do you know?

   Are you trusting him to lead you to accomplish his purposes? Why or why not?

2. What does it mean for you to be a Spirit-empowered witness in your world?

In what ways are you showing other people who God is as you conduct your daily life?

How do you receive from God the strength, encouragement, and guidance to be a witness?

What is necessary for you to become a more powerful witness of what God has done, and what is your commitment to do your part?

## A PENTECOST CHRISTIAN

- Asks God to indwell him/her in order to reflect God's presence to the world.
- Brings a spiritual harvest to God by testifying of him to other people.
- Demonstrates the presence of God's Spirit by caring for people in need.

## Closing (1 minute)

Read together Acts 2:38 – 39: "Peter replied, 'Repent and be baptized, every one of you, in the name of Jesus Christ for the forgiveness of your sins. And you will receive the gift of the Holy Spirit. The promise is for you and your children and for all who are far off — for all whom the Lord our God will call.'" Then pray, thanking

God for his willingness to dwell within everyone who believes. Ask him to live through you, to make the power of his presence overflow your lives and touch the hearts of people around you. Thank him for the privilege of bringing Jesus' presence into the world by speaking his words and demonstrating his presence to people who need him.

## Memorize

*Peter replied, "Repent and be baptized, every one of you, in the name of Jesus Christ for the forgiveness of your sins. And you will receive the gift of the Holy Spirit. The promise is for you and your children and for all who are far off — for all whom the Lord our God will call."*

*Acts 2:38 – 39*

# When Following Jesus Is the Most Important Thing in Life

*In-Depth Personal Study Sessions*

## Day One | God Is Faithful, Even When the Way Is Difficult

### The Very Words of God

> *I will sing of the LORD's great love forever; with my mouth I will make your faithfulness known through all generations. I will declare that your love stands firm forever, that you established your faithfulness in heaven itself.... You are mighty, O LORD, and your faithfulness surrounds you.*
>
> **Psalm 89:1 – 2, 8**

### Bible Discovery

### *The Disciples Find Their Lord to Be Faithful*

Imagine all that the disciples experienced from the time Jesus was arrested, through his crucifixion, until his ascension and the giving of the Spirit. As you think about their ups and downs, joys and sorrows, despair and joy, consider how your understanding of their journey of faith applies to your walk with God.

1. Immediately after Jesus' crucifixion, what was the mood of the disciples? (See Mark 16:8 – 14; Luke 24:1 – 4, 9 – 24; John 20:19.)

   What were they doing, and what had happened to their faith?

2.  How did the disciples' outlook change after they began to realize that Jesus truly was alive? (See Matthew 28:8 – 10, 16 – 17; Luke 24:36 – 43; John 20:19 – 20.)

3.  Despite the fact that he was leaving them, what impact did Jesus' ascension have on the disciples? (See Luke 24:50 – 53.)

    What do you think accounted for their change in attitude?

4.  How does Romans 5:2 – 5 help you to understand what was taking place in the hearts and lives of the disciples when they went back to Jerusalem to wait for God's power to come to them?

## Reflection

At one time or another, we all face seemingly impossible difficulties as we pursue our walk with God. We may feel that God has abandoned us. We may be confused as to what to do or which way to turn. As the disciples walked through the weeks before and after Jesus' crucifixion, they faced similar challenges. But through those difficult experiences, they found their Savior to be true and faithful. Based on him, they went out and changed their world.

In what ways has the disciples' journey of faith encouraged you to count on God's faithfulness when you face what seem to be impossible difficulties, when you don't know which way to turn, or when you feel abandoned by God?

What role does the Holy Spirit have in your life when you face difficulties that threaten to overwhelm you?

How confident are you that God will remain faithful to all of his promises and accomplish his work in your life no matter how desperate your circumstances may appear to be?

What do you think would increase your level of confidence?

How would you like Jesus' resurrection and ascension to make an even greater difference in *your* life, just as it made a huge difference in the lives of his disciples?

What is it you believe God wants you to go out into the world and accomplish for him?

How might what God already has done for you help you, or another person, to face difficult circumstances with peace, joy, and hope?

## Memorize

*We know that suffering produces perseverance; perseverance, character; and character, hope. And hope does not disappoint us, because God has poured out his love into our hearts by the Holy Spirit, whom he has given us.*

*Romans 5:3 – 5*

# Day Two | God Has Promised His Spirit

## The Very Words of God

*Because of your great compassion you did not abandon them in the desert. By day the pillar of cloud did not cease to guide them on their path, nor the pillar of fire by night to shine on the way they were to take. You gave your good Spirit to instruct them.*

*Nehemiah 9:19 – 20*

## Bible Discovery

### *God Manifests His Presence for His People*

God had allowed his presence to be physically evident in numerous ways prior to the birth of the church at Pentecost. Significant manifestations of God's Spirit occurred at the giving of the law to Moses, the establishment of the tabernacle, and the dedication of the temple built by Solomon.

1. In what ways was the Spirit of God evident while Moses and the people stood by Mount Sinai? (See Exodus 19:16 – 19.)

2.  How did God make his presence known in the Tent of Meeting, or tabernacle, during the Israelites' travels to the Promised Land? (See Exodus 40:34 – 38.)

3.  At the dedication of Solomon's temple, how did all of Israel know that God had taken up residence there? (See 2 Chronicles 5:7, 11 – 14; 7:1 – 3.)

4.  What did God promise Solomon regarding his ongoing presence in the temple? (See 2 Chronicles 7:11 – 12, 15 – 16.)

    How would this manifestation have contributed to the understanding of the temple (God's house) being a house of prayer?

5.  In what ways did God manifest his presence when the Holy Spirit moved from the temple building into the new temple — that of Jesus' disciples? (See Acts 2:1 – 5.)

## COMPELLING EVIDENCE

Consider the similarities between the manifestations of God's presence on Mount Sinai and those during Pentecost. Is it simply a coincidence?

| On Mount Sinai | During Pentecost |
| --- | --- |
| God's presence was accompanied by fire, smoke, and the sound of thunder (Exodus 19:16–19). | God's presence was accompanied by a sound like wind, tongues of fire, and the gift of languages (Acts 2:1–4). The Hebrew term translated "Holy Spirit," *Ruach HaKodesh*, means "Holy Wind." |
| When God gave the Torah to Moses, the people were worshiping the golden calf. About 3,000 people died as punishment for their sins (Exodus 32:1–4, 19–20, 27–28). | When Jesus' Spirit was given, many people repented and about 3,000 believed and found spiritual life (Acts 2:41). |
| God wrote the law on stone tablets (Exodus 31:18). | As he had promised, God wrote his law on the hearts of his people (2 Corinthians 3:3; Jeremiah 31:33). |
| God's presence was symbolized by a cloud and fire, which had led the Israelites out of Egypt. Later, God moved his presence into the temple (2 Chronicles 5:7–8, 13–14). | God's presence, evident in rushing wind and tongues of fire, moved from the temple into a new "temple"—the followers of Jesus (Romans 8:9; 1 Corinthians 3:16–17). |
| The Torah (*Torah* means "teaching") provided God's teachings for the Old Testament community of people. | The Holy Spirit became the Teacher of believers (John 14:26). |
| God met Moses—the Israelites' leader—on Mount Sinai, "the mountain of God" (Exodus 24:13). | Jerusalem was built on a mountain called "the mountain of the LORD" (Isaiah 2:3). |

## Reflection

God has been at work throughout human history, and at various times he has chosen to manifest himself to people so that they would know that he is the Lord, the all-powerful Creator, the one true God. Today, God has given his Spirit to those who believe on him so that other people will see that God is the one, true God.

In what ways has your understanding of the work of the Holy Spirit deepened as a result of this study?

If you are a Christian, the Holy Spirit dwells in you.

> What are the ways in which the Holy Spirit reveals himself to you?

> In which ways does the Holy Spirit teach you?

> How does the Holy Spirit help you to pray?

If you are a Christian, what does it mean for you to be the visible sign of God's presence to other people?

> How well do you represent God's presence to your family, friends, and community?

## Memorize

*Blessed are those who have learned to acclaim you, who walk in the light of your presence, O LORD.*

**Psalm 89:15**

# Day Three | Understanding the Meaning of Pentecost

## The Very Words of God

> *Then celebrate the Feast of Weeks to the LORD your God by giving a freewill offering in proportion to the blessings the LORD your God has given you.*
>
> *Deuteronomy 16:10*

## Bible Discovery

### Celebrate What God Has Given to You

Fifty days after Passover, at the end of the wheat harvest, the Israelites celebrated the Feast of Weeks (*Shavuot*) to honor God for his provision. According to the interpretations of Jewish religious leaders, *Shavuot* (Feast of Weeks) was also the day God gave the Torah on Mount Sinai. The history and practices of this celebration provide insights into what God was doing when he sent his Spirit upon the disciples on the morning of Pentecost.

1. God established the Feast of Weeks and revealed through Moses how it was to be celebrated. (See Leviticus 23:15 – 22; Numbers 28:26 – 31; Deuteronomy 16:9 – 12, 16.)

   a. When was it to take place?

   b. What were celebrants to present to God during the Feast of Weeks?

   c. Who was required to attend Pentecost — and the other two feasts — and appear before God in the temple?

2.  The Feast of Weeks was celebrated during the month Sivan — the third month. Which other significant event in Israel's history occurred during the third month? (See Exodus 19:1 – 6.)

3.  The Torah, which God gave to Moses on Mount Sinai, became the teacher for the Israelite community. On Pentecost, who became the teacher for the new community of Jesus' followers? (See John 14:23 – 26.)

How does recognizing that *Shavuot* celebrated in part the giving of the Torah (God's law or teachings) on Mount Sinai help you to understand why God planned the fulfillment of his promise to send his Spirit into his people to coincide with that celebration?

## DID YOU KNOW?

Although we often refer to the Torah as the Law of Moses, it actually means "teaching," not "law" in the way that Christians today might think. Although the Torah did provide "laws," or rules for life, it was not simply an organized collection of rules. The Torah was life itself. It was a vibrant message for life that was to be continually taught and applied to all situations.

4. Read the Scriptures that were read in the synagogue and temple about 9:00 a.m. on Pentecost, and list the subject of each. What insights do these readings provide concerning the events of Pentecost described in Acts 2?

| Scripture Reading | Subject |
|---|---|
| Exod. 19:1–20:26 | |
| Ezek. 1:22–28 | |
| The book of Ruth | |

## Reflection

Clearly God had the attention of his people at *Shavuot*. Jerusalem was crowded with faithful worshipers who:

- Were joyfully giving back to God an offering of what he had given to them
- Knew that God wanted them to share with other people who had unmet material needs
- Understood that God provided his teachings, his laws to live by, on Mount Sinai at *Shavuot*
- In the readings for that day, had just heard the prophet Ezekiel describe God in terms of wind and fire

Perhaps, then, it shouldn't surprise us that God chose that moment to do something new among his people.

In what ways does the biblical account of Pentecost come alive for you in light of the history of *Shavuot*? Write down several ways.

What new way of learning how to live for God was ushered in on Pentecost, and why is it as important for you (if you are a Christian) as the Torah was for the Jews on their way to the Promised Land?

Why do you think thousands of people became Christians soon after the Holy Spirit came upon Jesus' disciples?

In light of all that God has done — in providing for his people, in teaching his ways to live, in filling the disciples on Pentecost, in your life — for what do you want to thank him?

What do you want to give to him as an offering of firstfruits?

## DATA FILE

### Pentecost—The History of the Feast

The Feast of Weeks (also called *Shavuot*, in Hebrew; *Pentecoste*, by Greek-speaking Jews; and "the day of firstfruits") celebrated the end of the wheat harvest. It was a time to bring thank offerings to God and, according to Jewish tradition, the time when God gave Moses the Torah on Mount Sinai.

Instituted by God more than 1,200 years before Jesus sent his Spirit to indwell the disciples, the Feast of Weeks was one of three feasts during which all Jewish men were required to appear before God in the temple (Deuteronomy 16:16). It was an important enough feast for God-fearing Jews that the apostle Paul adjusted his itinerary in Asia Minor in order to arrive in Jerusalem by Pentecost (Acts 20:16).

The Feast of Weeks was celebrated fifty days after Passover Sabbath, hence, it was also called *Pentecost*, a word derived from the Greek word translated "fifty days." The faithful who celebrated Pentecost were to show concern for the poor by not harvesting the edges of their fields and by leaving the grain they dropped during the harvest (Leviticus 19:9–10; 23:22). They also invited the poor to a festive meal following the ceremony of offerings. God did not want those who came to him in gratitude to ignore those who were in need.

### Pentecost—The Birthplace of the Church

For Christians, Pentecost is considered to be the day when the Holy Spirit left the temple and came in visible, audible form and miraculously filled the disciples with God's power. It is the day on which the Christian church—the community of believers—was born.

Although Christians commonly believe that the disciples were in the upper room when they were filled with the Holy Spirit, that is unlikely:

- Crowds of people were present (Acts 2:5–6). These people would not have fit into a small room. Masses of people would have been in the temple on Pentecost.
- The disciples were continually in the temple (Luke 24:53) and would have been there on the day of Pentecost.

- Pentecost was one of the holiest days of the year, and it is likely that the disciples were in the temple for worship and to hear the readings at 9:00 a.m. (Acts 2:15).
- The disciples were in "the house" (Acts 2:1–2) when the Holy Spirit came upon them. Many Old Testament passages refer to the temple as "the house." However, the English translation is rendered "temple." (See Ezekiel 40:5, 42:15, and 43:10 in the King James Version.)
- Peter described his location as being near the tomb of David (Acts 2:29). According to 1 Kings 2:10, David was buried in the "City of David," the part of Jerusalem near the Temple Mount.

So where were the disciples when God's Spirit came upon them? No one knows for sure, but they were in the vicinity of the temple and perhaps in the temple courts or on the Southern Stairs where thousands of Jewish pilgrims would have gathered. Consider the evidence:

- The Southern Stairs led from the valley below, where David's City was located, to the double gates by the main processional entrance to the temple. Many thousands of pilgrims at a time walked up the Southern Stairs to the huge temple platform (about 900 by 1,500 feet) that surrounded the marble temple.
- The Southern Stairs were also known as the "Rabbi's Teaching Staircase" because they were a prime location for rabbis to teach their disciples. (Some scholars believe that Jesus' final discourse on the end of the world, found in Luke 21, took place as he left the temple by the Southern Stairs.) Listeners could sit on the broad, stone steps; passersby could gather and listen, too.
- Nearby ceremonial baths would have made it convenient for the disciples to baptize the approximately three thousand people who became believers after the Holy Spirit came upon the disciples. These baths were one of the few places where there would have been sufficient water to baptize that many people.

# Day Four | Abundant Generosity — the Evidence of Pentecost

## The Very Words of God

> *All the believers were one in heart and mind. No one claimed that any of his possessions was his own, but they shared everything they had. With great power the apostles continued to testify to the resurrection of the Lord Jesus, and much grace was upon them all.*
>
> Acts 4:32–33

## Bible Discovery

### Understanding the Generous Heart of God

Pentecost was a holiday of thanksgiving to God. The people brought to him the first of the harvest and demonstrated their thanksgiving by caring for needy people. God's mandate to be generous with one another and to the needy has never changed. He has a generous heart, and he still calls everyone who follows him to share his blessings with those who are less fortunate.

1.  Over and over again in Scripture, we read God's teaching concerning needy people. Caring for those in need is such an essential part of God's character that he required it to be part of the Feast of Weeks celebration of thanksgiving to him. As you read each of the following Scripture texts, note what it reveals about the generous heart of God and write down practical ways you could practice such generosity in your life.

| Scripture Text | The Generous Heart of God | How I Can Follow His Example |
|---|---|---|
| Exod. 22:25 | | |
| Deut. 15:11 | | |

| Scripture Text | The Generous Heart of God | How I Can Follow His Example |
|---|---|---|
| Deut. 24:14 | | |
| Ps. 35:10 | | |
| Ps. 109:30–31 | | |
| Prov. 22:22–23 | | |
| Jer. 22:16 | | |

2. In addition to bringing offerings to the temple, how were the celebrants of the Feast of Weeks (Pentecost) to show their thankfulness to God? (See Leviticus 19:9–10; 23:22.)

   What were they demonstrating about themselves and about God when they did this?

3. When the early Christians were filled with the Holy Spirit, how did they respond to one another and to the needs of other people? (See Acts 2:44–47.)

What were they demonstrating about themselves and about God when they did this?

## Reflection

God clearly cares about needy people, and he commands every Christian to help them. To love God is to obey him, and the Spirit leads God's people to bring his presence and power to bear on all who need his care. When God fulfilled his promise on Pentecost, the community of believers immediately began meeting one another's needs. They demonstrated that they were Spirit-filled by noticing needs and seeking to meet them — lovingly, generously, kindly, compassionately. We may never know the eternal difference we make when we help a needy person in the name of Jesus, but doing so always brings honor to God.

What does it mean when someone who claims to be a Christian (to be filled with God's Spirit) has no concern for people in need?

Do you view yourself as generous or stingy when it comes to helping needy people? Why?

What evidence of the Spirit's presence do you think other people see in your life? Is that what you want them to see?

Take a look at the list of ways you could follow God's example of generosity that you wrote in response to question one (see pages 278 – 279).

What specific action for a specific person could you do for each of these examples? How, for example, could you leave "gleanings" for a less fortunate person or family?

With which person will you begin honoring God's generous heart?

What kinds of needs should we — as Christians — be concerned about meeting for other people?

Whose needs will you seek to meet this week? This month? This year? What will you share?

## Memorize

*He who oppresses the poor shows contempt for their Maker, but whoever is kind to the needy honors God.*

*Proverbs 14:31*

## PENTECOST PROFILE
### Boaz—His Love for One Needy Person Changed the World

Each year on Pentecost, the Jews read the Old Testament book of Ruth. It tells the story of an Israelite couple who moved to Moab during a famine in Canaan. The husband and two sons died, leaving the mother (Naomi) and her two daughters-in-law alone. Naomi chose to return to Israel, and one of her daughters-in-law, Ruth, insisted on accompanying her.

Naomi had a relative on her husband's side named Boaz, and Ruth began picking up the barley left in his fields after harvest. Boaz had compassion on the destitute Gentile woman and provided generously for her. Eventually he became aware of his God-given responsibility and married her.

Little did Boaz know how the help he provided would change the world! Ruth had a son, who became the father of Jesse, who was the father of David—the lineage from which Jesus came! (See Matthew 1—the genealogy of Jesus.) By helping just one needy person in Jesus' name, we truly can make an eternal impact.

## Day Five | A Call to Spirit-Filled Living

### The Very Words of God

> *I will give you a new heart and put a new spirit in you; I will remove from you your heart of stone and give you a heart of flesh. And I will put my Spirit in you and move you to follow my decrees and be careful to keep my laws.*
>
> *Ezekiel 36:26–27*

### Bible Discovery

### God's Spirit Empowers Every Christian

Every Christian has been given God's Spirit to teach us and empower us to be his witnesses. By the power of the Spirit, we are to live in obedience to God. By his power we are to bring in the "spiritual harvest" as we share with other people the news of what God has done.

1. For what purpose did God give his power to his disciples on Pentecost, and how did people respond? (See Acts 1:8; 2:37 – 41.)

2. Who, other than Jesus' disciples at Pentecost, has been given the Spirit of God? (See Acts 5:32; Romans 8:8 – 9.)

3. What does the Spirit of God teach us? (See John 14:25 – 26; 1 Corinthians 2:11 – 12.)

4. In what ways does the Holy Spirit assist us in praying, and why is this important? (See Romans 8:26 – 27.)

5. What are some evidences of the Holy Spirit's work in our lives? (See Galatians 6:8 – 10; Ephesians 4:30 – 32; Philippians 2:1 – 4.)

God's desire for the Feast of Weeks (Pentecost) was for his people to be grateful to him for his provision and to care for people in need. In what way(s) does the work of the Holy Spirit in our lives fulfill God's intent for Pentecost?

## Reflection

God still desires that every Christian live a Spirit-guided life and become a person who pleases him, loves other people, and has a dynamic influence for his kingdom. Take some time to consider what it means for you to be a *Pentecost* Christian — one who is filled with God's Spirit, who is a witness for him, and who cares for people in need.

What evidence of the Spirit's presence is visible in your life? What is *not* evident?

Which change(s) might you need to make in order to truly demonstrate to other people the presence of God within you?

How committed are you to allowing the Holy Spirit to teach you so that the world may know the one, true God through you and the church — the complete body of Christians?

How do you obtain God's power so that you can live in obedience to him and be an effective witness?

With which persons might God want you, empowered by his Holy Spirit, to share his love and truth so they can develop a personal relationship with him and, in turn, reveal him to the world?

## Memorize

*All this I have spoken while still with you. But the Counselor, the Holy Spirit, whom the Father will send in my name, will teach you all things and will remind you of everything I have said to you.*

*John 14:25 – 26*

# TOTAL COMMITMENT

King Herod the Great, one of the most powerful people who ever lived in the land of Israel, was a construction genius. Appointed by Emperor Caesar Augustus to be king of Judea, he completed spectacular building projects that incorporated amazing features for that time in history — self-cleaning sewers, running water, a man-made harbor, a stadium, a palace hung on the edge of an 1,800-foot mountain, a freshwater swimming pool in the Mediterranean Sea, and an outdoor theater with engineered acoustics. To embellish these monumental accomplishments, he used the finest materials such as marble and gold and obtained the most skilled craftsmen to create magnificent mosaics, stonework, and frescoes.

Why did Herod build to such excess? He wanted to create a lasting legacy to himself.

This video focuses on what Herod built in Caesarea, a seacoast city named for the Roman emperor. The city was strategically located by the Via Maris at the northern end of the coastal plain of Israel. You'll view the ruins of Herod's man-made seaport — the largest of its time, even larger than the port of Alexandria — that made his realm a great commercial center. You'll see an aqueduct, amphitheater, and other impressive ruins and catch a glimpse of what life was like in that important city. As you explore all that Herod built, you will realize the importance of using your talents and energies to build the right things with your life.

The pagan city of Caesarea was Herod's crowning accomplishment. It was the entryway for the Roman worldview into the land of Israel. Although Herod had a self-serving perspective on life, God used what he accomplished in Caesarea to give early believers a launching point from which to share the message of Jesus the Messiah in the Gentile world. In Caesarea, where the humanistic views of Hellenism were widely accepted, the early believers first shared the gospel message of Jesus with non-Jews. That message went to both the common people and the region's influential leaders. Later, Caesarea became the gateway through which the gospel went out into the rest of the Gentile world. Christians today remember Caesarea primarily as the seaport through which Paul traveled during his missionary journeys.

Little of Caesarea's glory remains, however. The video will help you to visualize the stark contrast between the city's former splendor and its present ruins. Following a Jewish riot in AD 64, the Roman army came to the city to enforce Rome's domination. They considered Caesarea to be a "symbol of Jewish arrogance," so they virtually leveled it.

Today, one can find fragments of marble — the remains of Herod's genius — along the seashore. Such is his legacy. Most people remember him only as the cruel king who, in an effort to kill the baby Jesus (the king of the Jews mentioned in the prophecies of Scripture), ordered the death of all male babies in Bethlehem and the surrounding countryside. In contrast, small, water-worn stones remind us of the legacy of another person of the Bible: a youth named David who also became a great king of Israel. We remember him as the shepherd-warrior who killed a giant named Goliath with a common stone from a streambed so that "the whole world will know that there is a God in Israel"(1 Samuel 17:46).

## Opening Thoughts (4 minutes)

### The Very Words of God

> Brothers, you know that some time ago God made a choice among you that the Gentiles might hear from my lips the message of the gospel and believe.

*God, who knows the heart, showed that he accepted them by giving the*
*Holy Spirit to them, just as he did to us. He made no distinction between us*
*and them, for he purified their hearts by faith.*

*Acts 15:7 – 9*

## Think About It

Some people have a powerful drive to be successful and to leave a grand legacy to those who will follow. Talk about the different kinds of "monuments" to themselves that people build, and consider why some people devote so much time, money, and energy to doing this.

What do you think they are trying to achieve by building such monuments, and what is the lasting result?

# DVD Teaching Notes (18 minutes)

### The wonders of Caesarea

### Caesarea: gateway to the Gentiles for the gospel

### Legacies of stone: Herod and David

## DVD Discussion (7 minutes)

1. What were some of the remarkable features of Caesarea during Herod's time?

   Which cultural statements did they make to the world of Rome? To the world of the Jews? To the world of the early Christians?

2. As you saw what remains of Herod's great city and consider what he lived for, what did you think about what people today (including yourself) value in life?

3. What does the image of the two stones — the marble fragment and the ordinary sling stone — mean to you?

## DATA FILE
### The Glory of Caesarea — Wonder of the Ancient World
*The Harbor*

- No natural harbor existed, so Herod constructed a harbor using two break-waters. The south breakwater was 600 yards (1,800 feet) long; the north breakwater was 300 yards long.
- The base for these breakwaters was built of forty-foot by fifty-foot concrete blocks that were poured under water at depths up to a hundred feet.
- The towering lighthouse at the harbor entrance could be seen for miles.
- Harbor facilities included vaulted storage rooms along the breakwaters.

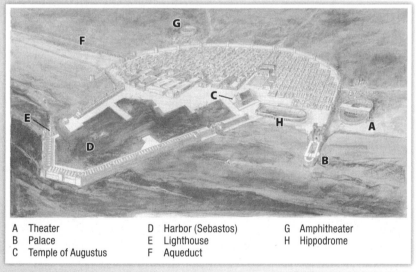

| | | |
|---|---|---|
| A Theater | D Harbor (Sebastos) | G Amphitheater |
| B Palace | E Lighthouse | H Hippodrome |
| C Temple of Augustus | F Aqueduct | |

**MAP OF CAESAREA**

*The Palace*

- Located on its own peninsula, the palace included a small port from which Herod's visitors could enter the palace from the sea without ever stepping into the city.
- The pool, a nature-defying "trademark" of Herod's palaces, was 115 feet long, sixty feet wide, and eight feet deep. It extended into the salty Mediterranean Sea, yet it most likely held fresh water.

*continued on next page . . .*

**THE REMAINS OF THE POOL IN THE PALACE AT CAESAREA**

- Herod welcomed his guests with luxurious rooms that included a large dining hall, hot and cold baths, and a semicircular colonnade that extended out into the sea.
- Most likely, Paul was imprisoned here for at least two years before he departed for Rome to appeal to the emperor.

### The Theater
- Located outside the city, probably because the bawdy and obscene performances that took place there were so offensive to Jewish residents.
- An important tool in promoting Hellenism, a lifestyle that glorified human knowledge, accomplishment, and experience.
- Positioned so that prevailing breezes provided amazingly good acoustics, the theater could hold about four thousand spectators who sat on stone benches.
- May have been the site where Paul presented his magnificent defense of the gospel to Felix, Festus, Agrippa II, and Bernice.

### The Temple of Augustus
- Dedicated to the goddess Roma and the "divine" emperor Augustus, it was one of the largest temples in the world at that time.
- Built on a great platform, the temple itself towered an additional one hundred feet.

- It was coated with plaster made from marble dust, which made it gleam white in the sun.

### The Hippodrome and Amphitheater

- It is not yet known if Herod built these facilities, but it is known that he promoted Hellenism by sponsoring sports festivals such as those that took place in such facilities.
- The games in these facilities were dedicated to pagan gods, were performed in the nude, and at times involved human bloodshed. They were considered by religious Jews to be immoral.

### The Aqueduct

- Provided the city and Herod's palace with water from springs on the slopes of Mount Carmel, since there was no fresh water source in Caesarea.
- Extended nearly nine miles from the city to the base of Mount Carmel, plus had an additional six miles of shafts and tunnels that burrowed into the mountain.
- An amazing engineering feat, it carried water in a plastered channel (much of which rested on a series of arches) across a river and through a channel cut into the sandstone hills.

**THE THEATER AT CAESAREA**

# Small Group Bible Discovery and Discussion (19 minutes)

## Caesarea — Where Gentiles First Received God's Spirit

After Jesus' ascension, his disciples received the Holy Spirit just as the Messiah had promised. From the moment they received the empowerment of the Spirit on Pentecost morning, they began to testify of what God had done. It is unlikely that they had any idea how soon God would reveal their role in taking the message of salvation to the Gentiles. It is even more unlikely that they imagined King Herod's seaport at Caesarea would be the gateway for sharing the message of Jesus to the Gentile world. As you explore the following passages, think about what you might have felt and thought if you were a Jewish believer or a God-fearing Gentile during this time in history.

1.  Acts 10 records a pivotal moment in the history of the Christian faith: the acceptance of believing Gentiles into the community of "circumcised" believers.

    a.  Who was Cornelius, where did he live, and what do we know about his lifestyle and religious beliefs? (See Acts 10:1 – 8.)

    b.  As Cornelius was responding to a message from the Lord, what unusual spiritual event was Peter experiencing? (See Acts 10:9 – 21.)

    c.  After Cornelius' messengers found Peter, what out-of-the-ordinary thing did Peter do? (See Acts 10:23 – 29.)

d.  For what purpose did Cornelius realize God had brought Peter to Caesarea? (See Acts 10:30–33.)

e.  What did Peter realize God was doing, and how did he reflect that in his message to the Gentiles who were with Cornelius? (See Acts 10:34–43.)

2.  Even though God was asking Peter and Cornelius to do things that were unheard of for men in their position, how did each of them respond?

To what extent were they surprised by what God was asking them to do, and how did they know that this new direction truly was from God?

What do you notice about their attitudes toward what God was doing, and toward one another?

3.  What amazing thing happened as Peter shared the message of Jesus with the Gentiles in Caesarea? (See Acts 10:44–48.)

How did the Jews who were with Peter respond, and why?

4. When God poured out his Spirit on the Gentiles, what happened within the early church? (See Acts 11:1 – 4, 15 – 18.)

   How did the community of Christians resolve this controversial situation?

   What do you learn from this situation that could help your faith community resolve controversies that arise, particularly controversies that arise out of ministry to people outside the traditional faith community?

## Faith Lesson (6 minutes)

Imagine how surprised the Jewish Christians were when God chose to pour out his Spirit on godly Gentiles in Caesarea. For so long, the Jews had benefited from their special covenantal relationship with the living God. Now, his unfolding purposes and love for Gentiles astonished some people, angered others, and certainly demonstrated that the world would never be the same.

1. In what ways did what God accomplished in Caesarea when he poured out his Spirit on the Gentiles change history — and our lives today?

2. To what extent are you open to new things that God is doing in the world?

   How do you respond, for instance, when people of different cultures, social status, or lifestyles come into your faith community?

3. How do you respond when God calls you into a situation or ministry that is way outside your comfort zone?

   How can you know that your calling is truly from God?

   What is your attitude toward doing something totally new? Are you eager? Fearful? Enthusiastic? Discontent?

## Closing (1 minute)

Read together Romans 10:12 – 13: "For there is no difference between Jew and Gentile — the same Lord is Lord of all and richly blesses all who call on him, for, 'Everyone who calls on the name of the Lord will be saved.' " Then pray, thanking God for the precious gift of his Spirit. Ask him to guide you and give you wisdom, just as he did the early church, when potentially divisive issues arise among Christians in your faith community. Invite him to fill you anew with his Spirit as you seek to follow him in all areas of your life and demonstrate to the world that he is the one, true God.

## Memorize

*For there is no difference between Jew and Gentile — the same Lord is Lord of all and richly blesses all who call on him, for, "Everyone who calls on the name of the Lord will be saved."*

*Romans 10:12–13*

# When Following Jesus Is the Most Important Thing in Life

*In-Depth Personal Study Sessions*

### **Day One** | The Herods: A Legacy of Rejection

### The Very Words of God

> *They perish because they refused to love the truth and so be saved. For this reason God sends them a powerful delusion so that they will believe the lie and so that all will be condemned who have not believed the truth but have delighted in wickedness.*

> *2 Thessalonians 2:10 – 12*

### Bible Discovery

### *Generations of Hardened Hearts*

Over the span of several generations, the Herod family had numerous encounters with the message of Jesus. One of those encounters was with Jesus personally, and others were with his passionate disciples. Although Scripture records no instance of anyone in this family believing in the Messiah, it does reveal some of the consequences of their unbelief — for innocent people as well as for themselves.

1.   Herod Antipas, son of Herod the Great, lived during the time of John the Baptist and Jesus, so he was well aware of their message and its impact on the people. How do we know that he opposed their message of repentance and redemption? (See Luke 3:19 – 20.)

2. Herod Antipas was the only Herod to actually meet Jesus face-to-face. What was his expectation of Jesus, and how did he respond when Jesus ignored him? (See Luke 23:8 – 11.)

3. How did Herod Agrippa, grandson of Herod the Great who built Caesarea, respond to the message of Jesus being spread throughout his realm? (See Acts 12:1 – 4.)

4. In what way did God thwart Herod Agrippa's plan? (See Acts 12:5 – 10, 18 – 19.)

5. How would you describe Herod Agrippa's relationship to God? What was the result of his attitude? (See Acts 12:21 – 24.)

6. What had Herod the Great done that no doubt influenced his grandson's perception of Jesus' message? (See Matthew 2:13 – 16.)

## FAMILY PROFILE
### The Legacy of the Herods: Generations of Hardened Hearts

| | |
|---|---|
| Herod the Great | Learned about Jesus' birth from the wise men; responded by trying to kill the infant Jesus (Matthew 2:1–16). |
| Antipas (Herod the Great's son) | Knew about Jesus; heard John the Baptist's teachings and had him arrested and later killed; met Jesus but sent him to Pilate (Mark 6:14–28; Luke 23:8–12). |
| Agrippa I (grandson of Herod the Great) to whom Emperor Claudius gave Herod the Great's entire kingdom. | Arrested Christians; had James put to death; imprisoned Peter; had to figure out how Peter escaped (Acts 12:1–5, 18–19); died when he allowed people to treat him like a god (Acts 12:21–23). |
| Drusilla (daughter of Agrippa I) | Listened to Paul as he spoke about faith in Christ Jesus (Acts 24:24–26). |
| Agrippa II (great-grandson of Herod the Great) | Discussed Paul's case in Caesarea with governor Festus; heard Paul's testimony; recognized that Paul was trying to persuade him to become a Christian (Acts 25:13–14, 23; 26:1–29). |
| Bernice (great-granddaughter of Herod the Great) | Accompanied Agrippa II and heard Paul's testimony (Acts 25:13–14, 23; 26:1–29). |

## Reflection

The legacy of rejection of Jesus' message by the Herod family clearly relates to our time and culture. All around us, people who are familiar with the claims of Jesus choose to defy him — quietly or publicly. Sometimes these people do whatever they can to hinder God's work on earth and slander his messengers. God, however, is watching. He will not allow his plans to be thwarted by any evil, and he will judge those who oppose him.

What does the example of Herod the Great's descendants say to you about the legacy each of us will leave?

To what extent do the values of parents and grandparents influence their children?

What effect did your grandparents and/or parents have on your response to God and his Word?

How closely have you examined the values you are passing down to future generations?

Why do you think no one in the Herod family believed Jesus' message?

For what reasons do people today refuse to believe his message?

Who do you know who has rejected God's message?

What have you done to present God's message to that person, and what will you continue to do?

When a person not only rejects God's message, but arrogantly defies God (as Herod Agrippa did), what are the consequences not only in the present but in the life to come?

## Memorize

*But for those who are self-seeking and who reject the truth and follow evil, there will be wrath and anger.*

*Romans 2:8*

## Day Two | Jesus' Testimony to a Shaper of Culture

### The Very Words of God

*"You are a king, then!" said Pilate.*

    *Jesus answered, "You are right in saying I am a king. In fact, for this reason I was born, and for this I came into the world, to testify to the truth. Everyone on the side of truth listens to me."*

    *"What is truth?" Pilate asked. With this he went out again to the Jews and said, "I find no basis for a charge against him. But it is your custom for me to release to you one prisoner at the time of the Passover. Do you want me to release 'the king of the Jews'?"*

*John 18:37 – 39*

# THE HEROD FAMILY TREE

### Antipater (Idumaean)

## HEROD THE GREAT

- Effective administrator, cruel, supported by Rome
- Visited by wise men, killed Bethlehem babies
- Greatest builder the ancient Near East ever knew
- Died in 4 BC
- Had 10 wives, three of whom were:

| Cleopatra | Miriam | Malthace |
|---|---|---|
| **PHILIP** | **ANTIPAS** | **ARCHELAUS** |

**PHILIP**

- Effective, popular king
- Ruled north and east of Galilee
- Built Caesarea Philippi

*(Luke 3:1)*

**ANTIPAS**

- Effective king
- Ruled Galilee and Perea
- Killed John the Baptist
- Built Tiberias and Sepphoris
- Tried Jesus before crucifixion

*(Matthew 14:1–12; Luke 3:19; 9:7–9; 13:32; 23:7–12)*

**ARCHELAUS**

- Poor ruler, deposed by Romans
- Ruled Judea
- Mary and Joseph settle in Nazareth to avoid him

*(Matthew 2:22)*

## HEROD AGRIPPA I

*(Grandson of Herod the Great)*

- King of Judea
- Killed James, put Peter in prison
- Struck down by an angel

*(Acts 12:1–24)*

**AGRIPPA II**

- King of Judea
- Paul defends his faith before him

*(Acts 25:13–26:32)*

**DRUSILLA**

└── *(Sisters of Agrippa II)* ──┘

- Married Felix, the Roman governor

*(Acts 24:24)*

**BERNICE**

- With her brother at Paul's defense

*(Acts 25:13)*

## Bible Discovery

### *Jesus Stands Secure Against Pilate's Questions*

Although he stayed in a palace in Jerusalem, Pilate actually lived in Caesarea, the Roman capital of Judea (Israel). He is credited with dedicating a temple in Caesarea to the Roman emperor Tiberius, so it is reasonable to assume that he was very Hellenistic and considered human reason to be his ultimate authority. The interaction between Jesus and Pilate provides fascinating insight into how Jesus affirmed his testimony, yet saw no need to answer even one of the charges brought against him.

1. Who was Pilate, and what questions did he ask Jesus? (See Matthew 27:11 – 14.)

   What amazed him about Jesus' answers and why?

   What differences do you think Pilate saw between the power he had as the Roman governor and the power wielded by Jesus, the alleged king who didn't even have an earthly kingdom?

   Who do you think was the more powerful person — Jesus or Pilate, and why?

2. What does the interaction between Jesus and Pilate in John 18:33 – 38 reveal about Jesus' desire to communicate with people in a way that encourages them to think for themselves and take action? What does it reveal about Pilate's Hellenistic view that truth is dependent on human reason?

3. To whom are Jesus' followers called to be witnesses? (See Matthew 28:19 – 20; Luke 21:10 – 15; Acts 1:8.)

   What insight do these passages give you into what Jesus may have understood his purpose to be and why he did not defend himself when he was before Pilate?

4. In what ways did Jesus manage to capture Pilate's interest (in kingdoms) and address his worldview (cynicism regarding truth) while Pilate was questioning him?

   What impact do you think Jesus' interaction may have had on Pilate long term?

   Do you think Pilate had unanswered questions he wished he had asked Jesus? If so, what do you think they would be?

## Reflection

Whether or not we realize it, each of us influences many people during our lifetime — family, friends, coworkers, students, community leaders, etc. Jesus' trials before the authorities of his day provide a powerful example of how one can stand for the truth and be a witness for God among people of influence.

How hard is it for you to stand up for what you believe and yet not be compelled to defend yourself at all costs when people attack you?

What have you learned in this regard from Jesus' example before Pilate?

Would you say that you are secure in your identity and your faith like Jesus was, or are you a bit like Pilate who was easily swayed by other people?

Hellenism, which in our culture is more commonly referred to as humanism, includes the belief that truth is dependent on human reason and therefore is constantly changing. To what extent has this worldview permeated your culture?

What ways have you found to reach out to or respond to people who are skeptical about Jesus and cynical about truth?

Do you truly believe that God can use you to influence people of all socioeconomic backgrounds — including people of influence?

What if, like Jesus and many of his disciples, you had to be arrested and put on trial in order to have a face-to-face meeting with culture shapers like Pilate?

## Memorize

*But in your hearts set apart Christ as Lord. Always be prepared to give an answer to everyone who asks you to give the reason for the hope that you have. But do this with gentleness and respect, keeping a clear conscience, so that those who speak maliciously against your good behavior in Christ may be ashamed of their slander.*

*1 Peter 3:15 – 16*

## Day Three | Caesarea — Launching Point to the Gentile World

## The Very Words of God

*So Saul stayed with them and moved about freely in Jerusalem, speaking boldly in the name of the Lord. He talked and debated with the Grecian Jews, but they tried to kill him. When the brothers learned of this, they took him down to Caesarea and sent him off to Tarsus.*

*Acts 9:28 – 30*

## Bible Discovery

### *The Gospel Goes Out through Herod's City*

The seaport Herod built in the cosmopolitan city of Caesarea played a vital role in spreading the news of Jesus throughout the Gentile world. Even though Herod built the seaport and expanded the thriving city solely to bolster his ego, improve his position with Rome, and glorify himself, God put what Herod had built to much better use.

1. In which Hellenistic city did Philip live and share Jesus' message? (See Acts 8:40; 21:8.)

2. How did Saul (Paul), a new follower of the Messiah, escape the Jews who were trying to kill him? (See Acts 9:28 – 30.)

3. How did the gospel first reach the Gentiles in Caesarea? (See Acts 10:1 – 2, 24 – 33, 44 – 48.)

   What irony might we see in this, in light of Herod's underlying motives for building Caesarea's amazing monuments? And in light of the occupational allegiance of Cornelius?

4. Note the role that Caesarea played in each of Paul's missionary journeys:

   Acts 9:30; chs. 13 – 14

## DATA FILE
### Why Caesarea? Why So Grand?

Herod built the seaport at Caesarea because he:

- Needed a port on the Mediterranean because existing ones were outside his kingdom or hostile to him.
- Recognized Caesarea's strategic location along the Via Maris, the trade route between Rome and such regions as Persia, Babylon, the Orient, and the Arabian Peninsula.
- Needed a vast source of revenue to fund his great building projects, such as the Temple Mount in Jerusalem and his palaces at Masada and Jericho.
- Sought to expand his influence, both to curry favor with Rome and to bring Roman culture and military support to Judea.
- Wanted to demonstrate his greatness.

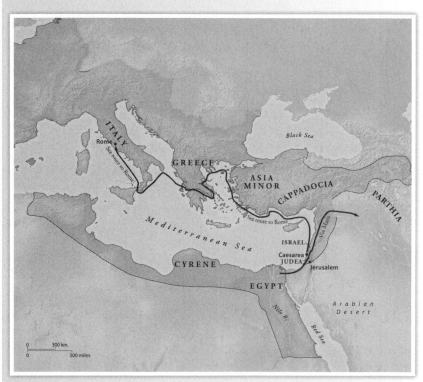

**THE ROMAN WORLD**

Acts 15 – 18


Acts 18 – 21


Acts 27 – 28


## Reflection

God accomplishes his plans in amazing ways, and sometimes the people and resources he uses are surprising. Think, for example, of how God used the prostitute Rahab to protect his spies before Israel crossed into the Promised Land. Think of how the idol of the Philistine god, Dagon, fell down before the ark of the covenant. Think of how the Babylonians were God's instrument to turn the hearts of his people toward him once again.

In what ways in modern life have you seen God use people who did not honor him, or man-made accomplishments, to fulfill his plans?


Which elements of your culture are used for evil, but also can be used to spread God's message?

How might you, or other Christians you know, make better use of these tools to show people who the one, true God is?

What specific things are you willing to do, during coming days and weeks, to be like Philip and further the kingdom of God in a pagan area?

As you think about your culture and which technologies are effective in reaching people, how might God want you to use those tools to further his kingdom and influence people who are not yet Christians?

## Day Four | Legacies of Two Kings

### The Very Words of God

> After removing Saul, he made David their king. He testified concerning him: "I have found David son of Jesse a man after my own heart; he will do everything I want him to do."
>
> **Acts 13:22**

### Bible Discovery

### Defined by Their Stones

Caesarea was but one of Herod the Great's magnificent projects. He built palaces in the desert, an enormous temple platform in Jerusalem, and a seaport harbor where there had been none. Yet today, all that is left of Herod's greatness in Caesarea are broken pieces of fine marble that wash up on the shore with the common stones. Herod lived to promote himself and to leave a grand legacy, but his seeming greatness and impact on history is of no consequence today.

In contrast, an Israelite boy named David used a common stone from a streambed and a powerful faith in the one, true God to kill a powerful giant. In this and many other battles fought on behalf of God's people, David brought honor to God and faith to God's people. What David did against Goliath in the Valley of Elah is a witness to what happens when a person uses his or her life to please and honor God. David's memory lives on.

1. For what reason was David willing to challenge Goliath, the giant soldier who taunted the Israelites and mocked their God? (See 1 Samuel 17:45 – 47.)

2. What effect did David's actions have on God's people, and how did God use him to bless all humankind? (See 1 Samuel 17:51 – 52; 18:6; Matthew 1:6 – 16.)

3. Fearful of losing his position and riches, Herod did whatever he could to survive and killed whomever might get in his way (Matthew 2:14 – 18). In contrast, where did David find strength, security, and hope to handle the difficult situations he faced? (See Psalm 18:1 – 2; 20:7; 25:4 – 5.)

4. How did God respond to David's faithfulness? (See 1 Chronicles 17:7 – 8.)

5. In contrast to King Herod, whose legacy lies in ruins today, how is David remembered? (See Matthew 1:1; Acts 13:22; 1 Peter 2:6.)

6. In what ways does Psalm 49:10 – 11 address what happened to the legacy of Herod?

## KINGS IN CONTRAST

| King Herod | King David |
|---|---|
| Tried to maintain his own security when facing real or perceived threats. | Trusted in God for his provision and guidance; brought his troubles before God in prayer. |
| Promoted Hellenism, a pagan worldview. | Promoted the one, true God. |
| Lived to promote his own glory. | Learned to honor God above all else. |
| Valued great wealth. | Valued his relationship with God above all else. |
| Paid homage to his patron, Caesar Augustus. | Honored God. |

## Reflection

Legacies are not just for kings. Each of us must choose whom we will serve and what kind of legacy we will leave. Will we seek fame, riches, control, power? Or will we dedicate ourselves to being obedient disciples of Jesus who serve him with all our heart, mind, soul, and strength? Will we, like Herod, use "stones" to build monuments to ourselves — or be like David who used his small sling-stones to

speak for God and build riches in heaven? Who or what will be lord
of our lives?

> Would you and other people who know you well say that you
> are using your "stones" — talents, abilities, resources, etc. — to
> build for yourself or for God and his kingdom? Why?

> What do you think is more important — what we build and how
> we build it, or for whom we are building it?

> If you could only pick up and label five "stones" to use in creat-
> ing your legacy, what would the labels say? Why?

> What practical difference should it make in your life that God
> can use such things as a small stone or an elaborate seaport to
> accomplish his work on earth?

> As you think about what kind of legacy *you* want to leave, what
> specific words would you like people to say about you after your
> death?

## Memorize

> *"Let not the wise man boast of his wisdom or the strong man boast of his strength or the rich man boast of his riches, but let him who boasts boast about this: that he understands and knows me, that I am the LORD, who exercises kindness, justice and righteousness on earth, for in these I delight," declares the LORD.*

> *Jeremiah 9:23 – 24*

# Day Five | Sharing Jesus at the Crossroads of Culture

## The Very Words of God

> *Pray also for me, that whenever I open my mouth, words may be given me so that I will fearlessly make known the mystery of the gospel, for which I am an ambassador in chains. Pray that I may declare it fearlessly, as I should.*

> *Ephesians 6:19 – 20*

## Bible Discovery

### Paul's Message for Agrippa II

Caesarea stood at the crossroads of culture, near the ancient trade route called the Via Maris. There, the first Christians shared the message of Jesus with powerful people who shaped their culture. Those first Christians were like standing stones. God placed them on the crossroads of the world so that their lives could point people toward God.

When speaking to Agrippa II — Herod the Great's great-grandson — and other powerful people in Caesarea, Paul spoke eloquently about a greater King for whom he was building an eternal legacy. What he said, and how he said it, reveals much about his personal commitment to God and his passion to reach people who were completely committed to the Hellenistic worldview that supported the Roman lifestyle of Caesarea.

In that pagan city, Paul — and other Christians — spoke and acted boldly, even though they were sometimes ridiculed and persecuted. As a result, many people around the world came to know Israel's God and his Son, the Messiah.

1. After Paul was accused by the Jews and arrested in Jerusalem, what circumstances led the Roman commander to arrange for Paul to go to Caesarea? (See Acts 23:12 - 24.)

   What did Paul boldly do there more than two years after his arrival? (See Acts 24:24 - 27.)

   What was Paul's message to the authorities who would hear him? (See Acts 25:13 - 26:23.)

2. How did Festus and King Agrippa respond to Paul's message? (See Acts 26:24 - 28.)

   What did they conclude? (See Acts 26:30 - 32.)

   In light of Jesus' words in Luke 21:12 - 15, how do you think Paul felt at this time?

## Reflection

In ancient Caesarea, where a spiritual war was being fought for the souls of people, God gave Paul a unique opportunity to share the gospel passionately with influential leaders. As you think about how God used events in Caesarea and the seaport there to promote his kingdom, determine how you might use today's technological advances to spread the gospel.

How serious are you about being God's witnesses to everyone around you — including powerful people in your community?

How does total commitment to living in obedience to God express itself in your life?

In what ways is a person's lifestyle essential to his or her message?

Does your lifestyle give you opportunities to speak your message? Why or why not?

Even as a prisoner, when people limited his sphere of influence, Paul used every opportunity to deliver the message of Jesus the Messiah to his world. What limits your sphere of influence?

Given that limitation, what opportunities do you have to share the gospel message?

How effectively are you using those opportunities?

Why do you think Paul was able to fearlessly present God's worldview everywhere he went rather than being afraid of the culture?

In what ways does Paul's refusal to be swayed by the agendas and accusations of others remind you of how Jesus faced his accusers?

What can you learn from their example about how to be uncompromising with the message regardless of whether or not it helps preserve your safety?

## Memorize

*I have fought the good fight, I have finished the race, I have kept the faith. Now there is in store for me the crown of righteousness, which the Lord, the righteous Judge, will award to me on that day — and not only to me, but also to all who have longed for his appearing.*

*2 Timothy 4:7 – 8*

# BIBLIOGRAPHY

## History

Connolly, Peter. *Living in the Time of Jesus of Nazareth.* Tel Aviv: Steimatzky, 1983.

Ward, Kaari. *Jesus and His Times.* New York: Reader's Digest, 1987.

Whiston, William, trans. *The Works of Josephus: Complete and Unabridged.* Peabody, Mass.: Hendrikson Publishers, 1987.

Wood, Leon. Revised by David O'Brien. *A Survey of Israel's History.* Grand Rapids: Zondervan, 1986.

## Jewish Roots of Christianity

Stern, David H. *Jewish New Testament Commentary.* Clarksville, Md.: Jewish New Testament Publications, 1992.

Wilson, Marvin R. *Our Father Abraham: Jewish Roots of the Christian Faith.* Grand Rapids: Eerdmans, 1986.

Young, Brad H. *Jesus the Jewish Theologian.* Peabody, Mass.: Hendrickson Publishers, 1995.

## Geography

Beitzel, Barry J. *The Moody Atlas of Bible Lands.* Chicago: Moody Press, 1993.

Gardner, Joseph L. *Reader's Digest Atlas of the Bible.* New York: Reader's Digest, 1993.

## General Background

Alexander, David, and Pat Alexander, eds. *Eerdmans' Handbook to the Bible.* Grand Rapids: Eerdmans, 1983.

Butler, Trent C., ed. *Holman Bible Dictionary.* Nashville: Holman Bible Publishers, 1991.

Edersheim, Alfred. *The Life and Times of Jesus the Messiah.* Peabody, Mass.: Hendrickson Publishers, 1994.

## Archaeological Background

Charlesworth, James H. *Jesus Within Judaism: New Light from Exciting Archaeological Discoveries.* New York: Doubleday, 1988.

Finegan, Jack. *The Archaeology of the New Testament: The Life of Jesus and the Beginning of the Early Church.* Princeton: Princeton University Press, 1978.

Mazar, Amihai. *Archaeology of the Land of the Bible: 10,000 – 586 B.C.E.* New York: Doubleday, 1990.

**To learn more about the specific backgrounds of this DVD series, consult the following resources:**

Avigad, Nahman. "Jerusalem in Flames — The Burnt House Captures a Moment in Time." *Biblical Archaeology Review* (November-December 1983).

Barkey, Gabriel. "The Garden Tomb — Was Jesus Buried Here?" *Biblical Archaeology Review* (March-April 1986).

Ben Dov, Meir. "Herod's Mighty Temple Mount." *Biblical Archaeology Review* (November-December 1986).

Bivin, David. "The Miraculous Catch." *Jerusalem Perspective* (March-April 1992).

Burrell, Barbara, Kathryn Gleason, and Ehud Netzer. "Uncovering Herod's Seaside Palace." *Biblical Archaeology Review* (May-June 1993).

Edersheim, Alfred. *The Temple.* London: James Clarke & Co., 1959.

Edwards, William D., Wesley J. Gabel, and Floyd E. Hosmer. "On the Physical Death of Jesus Christ." *Journal of American Medical Association (JAMA)* (March 21, 1986).

Flusser, David. "To Bury Caiaphas, Not to Praise Him." *Jerusalem Perspective* (July-October 1991).

Greenhut, Zvi. "Burial Cave of the Caiaphas Family." *Biblical Archaeology Review* (September-October 1992).

Hareuveni, Nogah. *Nature in Our Biblical Heritage.* Kiryat Ono, Israel: Neot Kedumim, Ltd., 1980.

Hepper, F. Nigel. *Baker Encyclopedia of Bible Plants: Flowers and Trees, Fruits and Vegetables, Ecology.* Ed. by J. Gordon Melton. Grand Rapids: Baker, 1993.

"The 'High Priest' of the Jewish Quarter." *Biblical Archaeology Review* (May-June 1992).

Hirschfeld, Yizhar, and Giora Solar. "Sumptuous Roman Baths Uncovered Near Sea of Galilee." *Biblical Archaeology Review* (November-December 1984).

Hohlfelder, Robert L. "Caesarea Maritima: Herod the Great's City on the Sea." *National Geographic* (February 1987).

Holum, Kenneth G. *King Herod's Dream: Caesarea on the Sea.* New York: W. W. Norton, 1988.

Mazar, Benjamin. "Excavations Near Temple Mount Reveal Splendors of Herodian Jerusalem." *Biblical Archaeology Review* (July-August 1980).

Nun, Mendel. *Ancient Stone Anchors and Net Sinkers from the Sea of Galilee.* Israel: Kibbutz Ein Gev, 1993. (Also available from *Jerusalem Perspective.*)

_____. "Fish, Storms, and a Boat." *Jerusalem Perspective* (March-April 1990).

_____. "The Kingdom of Heaven Is Like a Seine." *Jerusalem Perspective* (November-December 1989).

_____. "Net Upon the Waters: Fish and Fishermen in Jesus' Time." *Biblical Archaeology Review* (November-December 1993).

_____. *The Sea of Galilee and Its Fishermen in the New Testament.* Israel: Kibbutz Ein Gev, 1993. (Also available from *Jerusalem Perspective.*)

Pileggi, David. "A Life on the Kinneret." *Jerusalem Perspective* (November-December 1989).

Pixner, Bargil. *With Jesus Through Galilee According to the Fifth Gospel.* Rosh Pina, Israel: Corazin Publishing, 1992.

Pope, Marvin, H. "Hosanna: What It Really Means." *Bible Review* (April 1988).

Riech, Ronny. "Ossuary Inscriptions from the Caiaphas Tomb." *Jerusalem Perspective* (July-October 1991).

_____. "Six Stone Water Jars." *Jerusalem Perspective* (July-September 1995).

Ritmeyer, Kathleen. "A Pilgrim's Journey." *Biblical Archaeology Review* (November-December 1989).

Ritmeyer, Kathleen, and Leen Ritmeyer. "Reconstructing Herod's Temple Mount in Jerusalem." *Biblical Archaeology Review* (November-December 1989).

_____. "Reconstructing the Triple Gate." *Biblical Archaeology Review* (November-December 1989).

Ritmeyer, Leen. "The Ark of the Covenant: Where It Stood in Solomon's Temple." *Biblical Archaeology Review* (January-February 1996).

_____. "Quarrying and Transporting Stones for Herod's Temple Mount." *Biblical Archaeology Review* (November-December 1989).

Ritmeyer, Leen, and Kathleen Ritmeyer. "Akeldama: Potter's Field of High Priest's Tomb." *Biblical Archaeology Review* (November-December 1994).

Sarna, Nahum M. *The JPS Torah Commentary: Exodus.* New York: Jewish Publication Society, 1991.

"Sea of Galilee Museum Opens Its Doors." *Jerusalem Perspective* (July-September 1995).

Shanks, Hershel. "Excavating in the Shadow of the Temple Mount." *Biblical Archaeology Review* (November-December 1986).

"Shavuot." *Encyclopedia Judaica,* Volume 14. Jerusalem: Keter Publishing House, 1980.

Stern, David. *Jewish New Testament Commentary.* Clarksville, Md.: Jewish New Testament Publications, 1992.

Taylor, Joan E. "The Garden of Gethsemane." *Biblical Archaeology Review* (July-August 1995).

Tzaferis, Vassilios. "Crucifixion — The Archaeological Evidence." *Biblical Archaeology Review* (January-February 1985).

_____. "A Pilgrimage to the Site of the Swine Miracle." *Biblical Archaeology Review* (March-April 1989).

_____. "Susita." *Biblical Archaeology Review* (September-October 1990).

Vann, Lindley. "Herod's Harbor Construction Recovered Underwater." *Biblical Archaeology Review* (May-June 1983).

# *More Great Resources*
## *from Focus on the Family®*

### Volume 1: Promised Land

This volume focuses on the Old Testament — particularly on the nation of ancient Israel, God's purposes for His people and why He placed them in the Promised Land.

### Volume 2: Prophets & Kings

This volume looks into the life of Israel during Old Testament times to understand how the people struggled with the call of God to be a separate and holy nation.

### Volume 3: Life and Ministry of the Messiah

This volume explores the life and teaching ministry of Jesus. Discover new insights about the greatest man who ever lived.

### Volume 4: Death and Resurrection of the Messiah

Witness the passion of the Messiah as He resolutely sets His face toward Jerusalem to suffer and die for His bride. Discover the thrill the disciples felt when they learned of His resurrection and were later filled with the Holy Spirit.

### Volume 5: Early Church

Capture the fire of the early church with the faith lessons on Volume 5. See how the first Christians lived out their faith with a passion that literally changed the world.

### Volume 6: In the Dust of the Rabbi

"Follow a rabbi, drink in his words and be covered with the dust of his feet," says the ancient Jewish proverb. Come discover how to follow Jesus as you walk with teacher and historian Ray Vander Laan through the breathtaking terrain of Israel and Turkey and explore what it really means to be a disciple.

# *More Great Resources*
## *from Focus on the Family*®

### Volume 7: Walk as Jesus Walked — Making Disciples

The latest in-depth study once again takes viewers to Israel, where 12 disciples walked the walk their rabbi Jesus taught them. Examining the culture and politics of the first century, Ray Vander Laan opens up the Gospels as never before.

### The True Easter Story: The Promise Kept

Biblical historian Ray Vander Laan re-examines the dramatic events of Easter in The True Easter Story: The Promise Kept. New footage filmed in Israel, combined with earlier lessons from the series, show the death and resurrection of Jesus as a fulfillment of the promise God made to Abraham. Approximately 44 minutes; includes a bonus faith lesson, "Lamb of God."

### The True Christmas Story: Herod the Great, Jesus the King

Experience The True Christmas Story: Herod the Great, Jesus the King, filmed in Israel with expanded footage at the site of Herod's fortress. Biblical scholar Ray Vander Laan uses earlier lessons from the series to contrast the lives of Jesus and Herod, making the Christmas story even more meaningful. This 43-minute teaching includes a bonus faith lesson, "Living Water."

## FOR MORE INFORMATION

### Online:
Log on to www.focusonthefamily.com
In Canada, log on to www.focusonthefamily.ca.

### Phone:
Call toll free: (800) A-FAMILY
In Canada, call toll free: (800) 661-9800.

BD08XTTWMK